Single, Again, and Again, and Again . . .

What do you do when life doesn't go to plan?

LOUISA PATEMAN

BALBOA.PRESS
A DIVISION OF HAY HOUSE

Balboa Press books may be ordered through booksellers or by contacting:

Balboa Press
A Division of Hay House
1663 Liberty Drive
Bloomington, IN 47403
www.balboapress.com.au
1 (877) 407-4847

Because of the dynamic nature of the Internet, any web addresses or
links contained in this book may have changed since publication and
may no longer be valid. The views expressed in this work are solely those
of the author and do not necessarily reflect the views of the publisher,
and the publisher hereby disclaims any responsibility for them.

The author of this book does not dispense medical advice or prescribe the use
of any technique as a form of treatment for physical, emotional, or medical
problems without the advice of a physician, either directly or indirectly. The
intent of the author is only to offer information of a general nature to help
you in your quest for emotional and spiritual well-being. In the event you use
any of the information in this book for yourself, which is your constitutional
right, the author and the publisher assume no responsibility for your actions.

Any people depicted in stock imagery provided by Getty Images are
models, and such images are being used for illustrative purposes only.
Certain stock imagery © Getty Images.

Print information available on the last page.

ISBN: 978-1-5043-2138-9 (sc)
ISBN: 978-1-5043-2139-6 (e)

Balboa Press rev. date: 05/07/2020

ACKNOWLEDGEMENTS

Thank you, Laura, for encouraging me to tell my story and convincing me this was the book to write.

To Zoe—I am eternally grateful for your unwavering support, even when I am painful and unbearable. You have never given up on me.

And Maxine and Judy, you are my rocks, together forever, through thick and thin.

INTRODUCTION

Do you ever feel like you'll never find *the one*? Are you sick of failed relationships? Do you feel like you are the only single woman left on the planet? And are you seriously fed up with comments from friends and family hinting that you are getting old and need to settle down before it's too late?

Well, that's how I felt. At thirty-six, I was constantly being reminded of how my time was running out; I needed to get married and have children. Like it was that simple! Like I had a wand I could wave and magically create a husband! I was single and felt I had no control over my predicament. After all, I was only half of the equation. I wasn't on my own for lack of trying, and regardless of what people assumed, it wasn't entirely my fault!

My close friends and family gave me gentle nudges and kind reminders that my childbearing years were nearing the end and I should get a wriggle on. I didn't need their reminders. My biological clock was ticking loud enough for the whole neighbourhood to hear. I felt panicked and alone.

As young girls, we grow up with society laying out our life plan: get a good job, get married, and have kids. After all, our primary purpose is to procreate. Simple! But what happens if that predetermined path doesn't appear?

Until you have walked in the shoes of a single, childless woman over the age of thirty-five, you can't know the pressure, the sadness, and the disappointment of trying to fulfil your life's purpose and falling short; wanting desperately to find the right man and grow a family together. Unless you have experienced it, you have no idea of the depths of loneliness or the trauma generated by constant rejection. And then there is the frustrating pity from friends and family as they look upon your plight with dismay.

In my thirties, I found myself avoiding my couple friends, as being with them was too uncomfortable. I felt like a third wheel, and I didn't want to be reminded of what I didn't have. As a single woman, I was treated differently, like a misfit. I was segregated from the respectable twosomes, often left out of social gatherings, and given a separate table at weddings and special events. It was like I had developed a disease. I was an outcast who didn't quite fit social norms.

With the best of intentions and intense determination, I tried to find my soulmate and dutifully fulfil society's expectations of me. But it didn't quite go to plan.

This is my story: a synopsis of my journey, trying to the best of my ability to accomplish my preset life path. It is based on my recollection of events, through my eyes, and from my perspective. It is my view of my world. I have no doubt that some of the people whose paths I have crossed may have different versions of these events, since they possess different filters and carry a different perspective. I have tried to stay authentic and true to the events as they occurred.

To safeguard the identity of others, I have, in some circumstances, omitted certain details, if I felt these were not necessary to orchestrate my story. I have changed people's names and sometimes locations to protect privacy. And after instruction from my publisher, I have changed my name as well. But the stories are real.

To be clear, I do not profess to be an expert on any topic discussed in this memoir. I am just an ordinary woman who, incidentally and without intending to, built an extraordinary life out of her perceived failures.

CHAPTER 1

The Life Plan

When I was eleven, I discovered boys.

Sure, I had played the odd game of catch-and-kiss on the playground, but reluctantly, under extreme duress, accepting only a kiss on the back of my hand. And I did have my first innocent crush on a boy who was good at maths when I was nine. But for the most part, I didn't waste much energy thinking about boys. I was happy riding my bike, climbing trees, and playing with my brother, who was a year older than me.

Until I turned eleven.

I was in primary school when some of the girls started getting boyfriends. Out of nowhere, our conversations were infiltrated with talk about boys and who had a crush on whom. Getting a boyfriend was like winning a prize. Being asked by a boy to "go out with him" was a real achievement. It was the unofficial schoolyard rating system, the popularity test. We were very young—only just coming into puberty. After holding hands for a few weeks, couples would break up, and new couples would form. It was a new era.

Over the next few years, as my body changed, so did my thoughts. I spent more and more time thinking about boys, about love, and about what I wanted for my future. Thus began my fantasies about what it would be like to have someone special and be in love.

Grooming

Unbeknownst to me, my fantasies were the product of years of grooming. As a child, I had read many of the classic fairy-tale books. I watched fairy tales depicted in cartoons, and I listened wholeheartedly to the fantasy love stories read to me by my mother at night.

I loved hearing about Snow White and her adoring dwarves, who was tormented by her wicked stepmother. Miraculously she was rescued by a charming prince whom she married and together they lived happily ever after. I also enjoyed learning about Rapunzel, who was imprisoned by an evil witch inside a tower in the woods and then discovered by a charming prince, whom she later wed and went on to live happily ever after. Then there was Sleeping Beauty, who was cursed by an evil fairy and forced to spend years in a deep sleep waiting for her curse to be broken by her true love's kiss. She was gallantly rescued by her charming prince, and they also went on to get married and live happily ever after.

There were many stories with similar themes, but my favourite story, the story that inspired me the most, was Cinderella. What an amazing transformation—the rags to riches, the wrong made right, and the toppling of another evil stepmother. All was made possible from just one night of romance, during which the handsome prince, her saviour, falls madly in love with her. Henceforth, Cinderella goes on to get married and, of course, live happily ever after.

The fairy tales all had a recurring theme: a young lady, often beautiful, trapped in a torturous circumstance, is found and rescued by a handsome and charming prince. Unquestionably, they fall in love and live happily ever after. The prince we never really knew anything about. Beyond being handsome and charming, was he a good person? Was he intelligent? Was he a good communicator? What were his best attributes? I never really did figure that out. He had money and status, and no other details were important enough to mention.

The two events were interdependent: being rescued by the charming prince and living happily ever after. To be happy, the damsel in distress needed to marry the prince. End of story.

"Happily ever after" is such a sweeping statement. What does it even mean? Supposedly it refers to a married couple with children living blissfully together in perfect harmony, without stress or adversity. It is a notion of everlasting love, implying that everything will work out perfectly in the future.

Understandably, from a very young age, I was in pursuit of my own happy ending. Just like every other little girl, I wanted my happily-ever-after. Perhaps, though, I had been misled.

Nowadays, there is much debate about the negative repercussions of a young girl's obsession with seeking her happily-ever-after. Some suggest that such a heavy burden may cause psychological impairment. Sadly, I wasn't blessed with this perspective when my life plan was taking shape.

And why are the villains in these fairy tales often a woman? Why is there often an evil stepmother? The fairy tales all portray the second wife as a woman who is uncaring, unloving, and fuelled by jealousy. This certainly doesn't make it easy to send positive messages about blended families. The stories imply this subsequent wife is not capable of embracing another woman's child. Upon reflection, this is not a constructive subliminal message.

Ironically, in these fantasy love stories, there is no mention of the psychological damage endured by the damsel in distress, no mention of post-traumatic stress disorder, no mention of the countless visits to psychologists necessary to work through her lifelong issues. The mere presence of the prince is a magical antidote that cures all.

There was no inference of Cinderella needing therapy after years of emotional and physical abuse, and there was no discussion of counselling for Rapunzel after her years in solitude. Not to mention Snow White second-guessing her own character-assessment capabilities after naively accepting gifts from strangers that almost caused her death. Any and all suffering wondrously disappeared at the hands of the prince. It magically disappeared, and they all lived happily ever after.

The fairy-tale damsels, it appeared, had no control over their future. Their prosperity hinged on the arrival of a man.

Entrenched in my subconscious mind, these fairy tales would later guide me on my own search for happiness. The terms of reference were set, and the instructions were clear: I just had to find my prince, and *voila*, my happily-ever-after would automatically ensue.

<u>Society's Cues</u>

The grooming didn't stop with fairy tales. Society also played a role. There was never any doubt in my family's mind that a young girl's destiny was to grow up, get married, and start a family. This destiny had been clear since the dawn of time, or so it seemed. Biologically, I was designed to reproduce, so it made sense that my fate was to get married and bear children. Of course, there was a suggestion that I might find a good job somewhere on my journey, but the end goal was pretty clear.

Society's cues came from many sources, including movies, magazines, religious discussions, and general conversation. A continual flow of verbal and nonverbal cues was everywhere around me as I grew up. Every good love story ended with the girl getting the guy. Regardless of the hurdles in front of her, the leading lady always found her man. Society ignited in me, and in every other little girl, a love-story fantasy, a fabricated dream.

The message was unmistakable: the measure of my life's success was to get married and have children. And just like that, my beliefs were formed. There was only one path for me to follow, one prewritten script, one life plan.

<u>Teenage Years</u>

In my teens, my girlfriends and I spent many hours talking about boys, thinking about boys, and dreaming about boys. And we had many memorable adventures centred around chasing boys. I was especially close to Maxine and Judy, as I affectionately called them (more on that later). From the age of fourteen, they were my two best friends—my BFFs. We were inseparable.

The three of us met through our love of playing netball. Maxine went to a Catholic all-girls' school, while Judy and I attended the local coed public high school, although we didn't share many classes together. We each lived within walking distance of the neighbourhood park, which featured a playground, sports field, and tennis courts. After school, we would make our way to the park, our regular meeting point, to hang out. It was here we spent many hours together. It was during an age when mobile phones didn't exist, and our parents allowed us to stay out until dark.

Our friendship was solid. We were three very different girls who thoroughly enjoyed each others' company. I used to liken us to the points of an equilateral triangle, because we each had our own distinct way of being. Judy was kind and caring, Maxine was gregarious and defiant, and I was studious and sensible. We loved each other, and we laughed about our differences.

Ironically, we had loathed each other in earlier years. Maxine and I had played against each other in opposing netball teams. Both very competitive, we were arch-enemies on the court. Similarly, it was my competitive nature that caused an earlier rift with Judy. During a school basketball game, Judy took it upon herself to deliberately trip me because she felt I was being too competitive and taking the game far too seriously (well, that's my recollection). I landed flat on my face and subsequently held a grudge against her for years.

I look back now and laugh at those times. How amusing that I would form a lifelong friendship with two girls who had been my enemies.

On weekends, the three of us would gather in Judy's lounge room with a dog called Buddy (who suffered from an unfortunate flatulence problem) and watch chick flicks and tragic love stories, while eating oven fries with ketchup and way too much salt. We fell in love with different actors playing characters in the movies— John Cusack, Keanu Reeves, Patrick Swayze, and Tom Cruise—and indulged in the idea that we too would one day get our serendipitous love story.

We especially loved watching *Lace*, the story of three best friends and their schoolyard pact to stay together through '*thick and thin*', a motto we adopted for ourselves. It followed the journey of Maxine, Judy, and Pagan through a teenage pregnancy and many relationship make-ups and break-ups. We loved this story and how the characters freakishly resembled our own identities. Our looks even paralleled our counterparts'. We delighted in comparing our own journeys with those of the characters and often called each other by our replicas' names.

Sometimes, however, the whole boy obsession became too much for me. Being the sensible one in our threesome, I had to question some of the insane ideas the girls would dream up to chase boys.

For example, I had to draw the line one night when five of us had a sleepover at Renee's house, another friend from school. We were fifteen years old. The girls devised a grand plan to meet a group of boys at the neighbourhood park around midnight. Remember, we weren't blessed with the technology of mobile phones back then. It was a time when you had to make a firm commitment and stick to it.

The midnight plan didn't bode well with my sensibilities. I chose to resist peer pressure and stay behind at Renee's house. The genius plan involved the four girls sneaking out of Renee's bedroom window while I was left alone to calm the barking dog. Once Renee's mum fell asleep, the girls arranged their pillows to replicate sleeping bodies under the blankets and then snuck out the window. I was glad I wasn't with them. I was not interested in the neighbourhood boys and just wanted to get some sleep.

Twenty minutes later, while I was still trying to calm the nuisance dog, the home phone rang. Shortly after, Renee's mum entered the bedroom. Pretending to be awakened and startled, I watched as she discovered the four girls were not in their beds. It turned out Maxine's mother was bizarrely sitting on her porch at midnight that night and saw four teenage girls strolling past her house. After a laughable escapade (in hindsight), the girls' were caught out.

There was a bright side: my decision to stay back on my own that night earned me significant brownie points with all the mums. My star rating rose, and after her months of grounding, Maxine was only ever allowed out in the evenings if I chaperoned her. As a dutiful friend, I couldn't say no, even when I wanted to.

We rode the roller coaster of our teenage years together. These were exciting times. Through boyfriends and break-ups, we made some wonderful memories and stuck together through thick and thin.

My teenage years, though, weren't always about boys. I was doing well at school, which I enjoyed. And I also managed to get a part-time job and spend quality time with my family.

Creation of the Life Plan

After finishing high school, I was accepted into a university in Sydney, almost two hours from home via public transport. Maxine and Judy followed a different path, securing full-time jobs in the city centre. We managed to stay close despite the distance between us. It was a time of change and the beginning of a new life chapter.

By the age of nineteen, I had moved out of home and was learning to be independent. I was on my way to getting a university degree. I was ticking boxes left, right, and centre. My future was taking shape, and everything seemed to be on track—everything, that is, except my love life.

I knew I had plenty of time to settle down, but the thought still nagged at me from the back of my mind. I secretly wanted a strong, intelligent, and kind man to fall madly in love with me, propose to me in the most obscure and romantic way, marry me, and have children with me one day. I wanted to know it was going to happen— maybe not now, but definitely before I turned thirty. Thirty just seemed so old!

Thereupon I forged my first life plan. Not a lot of thought or rationale went into this plan; it was just a basic timeline to ensure my future happiness. The girls and I often laughed about the plan. It was a fun reminder of what lay ahead.

Life Plan #1

1. Find a suitable man by the age of 23
2. Fall in love
3. Be in a relationship for at least 2 years
4. Get engaged
5. Get married by the age of 26
6. Have my first child at 27
7. Have my second child at 29
8. Turn 30
9. Live happily ever after.

Soulmate, the One, the Right Man

My life plan seemed simple enough. Surely I could manage to accomplish my tasks in due time. Easy! Or was it? Upon reflection, I realised some complexities were missing from the plan, for society had already ingrained in me a notion that I wasn't just looking for a suitable man, I was actually looking for the *perfect* man.

So who was this perfect man? A mysterious figure also referred to as the *right man, Mr. Right, the one,* or *soulmate*—different terms to describe the same concept. A concept that implies there is precisely one person who is the perfect match for each of us. Just one!

The responsibility to find the one right man for me was seriously daunting. From a mathematical perspective, my task was to find one perfect man among nearly six billion people on the planet. Now, to be fair, only half are men, so assuming my one man would fit within a fifteen-year age bracket, it was more like one perfect man in half a billion, or some other ridiculously huge number. It was a degree of difficulty beyond comprehension.

This perception of "just one" invoked in me a small degree of anxiety and a touch of fear. With a deadline of thirty and half a billion men to sift through, was there anything else I needed to add to the equation? Yes, there was one more complication: the layer of serendipity, the romantic notion that life will happen by chance.

Effectively, good fortune and luck were required to make my happily-ever-after. I needed to have faith that my soulmate would cross my path at the right place and the right time.

So, when my mysterious soulmate crossed my path, how would I know he was actually the one? For such an important life decision, I wanted to be sure. The whole notion baffled me.

I decided to go right to the source and ask married family members how I would know when I had met *the one*. More often than not, their response was, "You just know." What on earth did that mean? "You just know." How was that a helpful answer? It was vague and dismissive, suggesting that my married respondents didn't really have the answer. It perplexed me how the heck they had made their decision to even get married.

I wanted a checklist—a proven checklist, not some made-up guesswork. I wanted to know for sure when I had found *the one*. I wanted all the variables. What did I need to tick off to satisfy myself that a potential suitor was truly my soulmate? With centuries of love stories, why was there no explicit algorithm?

The advice I received was seriously unhelpful. I would rather have been told, "Well, actually, you never really know if you've met *the one*; you just convince yourself it's right." That answer would have been more helpful. But those I interviewed did not want to admit to an impressionable young lady that they had married someone who potentially wasn't their soulmate—that they settled for something less than perfect. Instead, the myth that marriage was the union of two perfectly matched souls was etched into my mind. My beliefs were solidified.

The pressure to choose the right one made my life-plan quest seem overwhelming. Like climbing Mount Everest, the pursuit seemed impossible. My other life challenges seemed to be a breeze in comparison.

CHAPTER 2

Entering My Twenties

Excitedly, I entered my twenties: the decade before I turned old, the decade in which I was supposed to meet my soulmate and start my happily ever after. My twenties did afford me a lot of first-time life experiences. I finished university and embarked on my first professional job. I bought my first property, and I travelled overseas for the first time. I hit goals in many aspects of my life—except, of course, the elusive ultimate goal.

<u>Almost the One</u>

By the age of twenty, I had sifted through a few duds in search of *the one*. I say *dud* in jest, as I was indeed very fortunate to date some lovely young men, but for a range of reasons, the relationships failed. Nonetheless, I termed them *duds* since clearly none of them was the right man for me.

Then I came close to accomplishing my life plan—or so I thought. I met a new potential: Ross. He stood out as intelligent and an excellent communicator, and slightly aloof. Over the next two years, we enjoyed many special times together. My friends and family adored him, and I was in love. I was optimistic I had found *the one.*

Ross and I met and dated whilst I was at university, a time when I was very close to my aunt and uncle. Aunty and Uncle, as I called them, were two generations older than me. Aunty was my grandmother's sister, and Uncle was my grandfather's cousin. They were the two people in my life whose opinion mattered most to me.

For most of my teenage years, I lived with Aunty and Uncle. In their sixties, they were retired and spent their leisure time growing an enormous vegetable garden and raising backyard chickens. Uncle played lawn bowls every Wednesday, and Aunty spent most of her day cooking. She also spent hours on end ironing clothes. Everything got ironed, and I mean *everything.* After countless melted holes in my synthetic underwear, my aunt kept ironing them. It was a pastime she thoroughly enjoyed.

These two beautiful people were instrumental in setting my values. They were loving and nurturing and had very robust ideas on marriage. They had been happily married for over fifty years, and they were great role models. After half a century, they still laughed together, respected each other, and supported one another. They set the bar high and offered big shoes to fill.

Sadly, they couldn't bear children—something that haunted them their entire life. Aunty often described her despair at not being able to have babies. She felt she hadn't fulfilled her purpose in life; she had no legacy to leave. Even though decades had passed, this was an open wound that never healed. She was sad inside.

My entrance into their life was mutually beneficial. My presence gave them a purpose—a child to love, mould, and shape, someone to pass on a legacy. I became someone for them to be proud of, to invest in. Uncle would boast about my achievements to his mates at the bowls club. I gave him a smile, and I gave him a reason to live.

And the benefits were reciprocal. They gave me love, and they gave me guidance. I can never thank them enough for their role in my life.

Aunty would often call me Pollyanna after a character in an old black-and-white movie who comes to live with a cranky old aunty and shows the woman how to love. Aunty wasn't cranky, but there were times when I did push her past her limits.

I was a cheeky child who brought them entertainment. In the vegetable patch after school, I would sometimes grab the watering hose and chase my sixty-five-year-old aunt around the garden. I found it so funny! She would just shake her head at me with pursed lips in a defeated smile. Each afternoon, I would collect the freshly laid eggs and snap off a cob of corn to eat raw while I talked to them about my day.

Aunty and Uncle believed their duty was to set me up for adulthood. They were always incredibly impressed by my educational successes, but they were more focused on other things. They dearly wanted me to find someone and get married. They emphasised the importance of meeting someone while I was young enough that we could grow together, young enough that I was not yet set in my ways. They only wanted what they believed was best for me: to find a husband, settle down, and have children.

Moving away from home to attend university was exhilarating and rewarding, but it did put me over an hour's drive from my school friends and my aunt and uncle. The distance didn't matter; I went home most weekends, and my underwear continued to get ironed.

Uncle had been battling cancer for almost a decade, and his dream was to walk me down the aisle before he passed. He had seen me graduate from university and settle into my first professional job. He was happy I was in a relationship and felt his baby girl was on the right path.

I remember walking into Uncle's bedroom one day. I was twenty-three years old. By this time, his cancer had spread, and he was bedridden with twenty-four-hour care. I remember it so clearly: walking into the room, the brown-and-gold-flecked shag pile carpet on the floor, the gold-and-cream printed wallpaper, the dark-brown-veneer bedroom suite. Uncle was lying in bed as I walked over to kiss him goodbye before heading home. He held my hand, looked me in the eyes, and, in a very soft voice, said, "Anytime Ross wants to ask me." Hinting that he didn't have much longer to live, so I might want to prompt Ross to ask permission for my hand in marriage before it was too late.

At that moment, my heart broke. I gave my uncle a warm smile and shrugged off his suggestion. "Oh, Uncle," I muttered. Inside, my heart was torn in two. I desperately wanted to give my uncle his dying wish to see his baby girl get married. I wanted to provide him with hope and peace of mind. But sadly, my relationship with Ross wasn't even close to being permanent. In fact, it was quite the opposite. Ross had other plans. After two-and-a-half years together, he had just confessed he was young and wanted to "experience other women."

Sadly, my uncle did not get his dying wish, nor did my aunt. They both passed when I was in my twenties and the furthest I could be from marriage.

Only Allowed Three

The subtle pressure from the family didn't end with Aunty and Uncle. I was heavily influenced by other relatives.

In my twenties, I spent time with another family couple who were younger—in their thirties. They were happily married with two young girls, and of course, they expected that my path would involve marriage and children. Concerned about the impression I might bestow upon their daughters, I was on strict instructions to introduce a maximum of only three men to the family. Just three! Supporting old-fashioned values, their rules were not negotiable.

They adored Ross and were bitterly disappointed when our relationship ended. I felt like I had failed them. Not only was I coming to terms with my break-up, but I also had to grapple with the feeling that I'd disappointed many of my family members. Alas, one down, only two more introductions allowed.

Return to Single Life

Finding myself single at twenty-three, I needed to amend my life plan. It just needed a few tweaks. I gave myself another couple of years to find Mr. Right. All good; I still had plenty of time.

Life Plan #2

1. Find my soulmate by the age of 25
2. Fall in love
3. Be in a relationship for 1 year
4. Get engaged
5. Get married by the age of 27
6. Have my first child at 28
7. Have my second child at 29
8. Turn 30
9. Live happily ever after.

Perfect!

Re-entering single life, I was surprised how things had changed since my teens. Most of my girlfriends were now settled into steady relationships. Maxine was engaged, and Judy was travelling overseas, meeting her future husband.

My social life now entailed going out with couples. I officially became the third wheel. I would be sitting at a restaurant as my couple friends whispered in each other's ears, giggling at their secret innuendos. They had their someone special, and I got to sit and watch what I didn't have. I was grateful for the company, and I was thankful for the opportunity to get out of the house, but I didn't feel like I fitted in. I kept my head held high, but I was secretly sad, and I was secretly lonely.

It was during this time I was reminded how important my task of finding my soulmate was, for I was bombarded with a barrage of questions only related to finding a husband.

"How's your love life?"

"Have you met anyone?"

"Is there anyone you fancy?"

Question after question, solely related to my pursuit of *the one*. Despite the fact that I had managed to get a university degree, relocate to a new city, and save a deposit to buy my first property—all worthy achievements to be talked about and celebrated—none of these accomplishments featured much in conversation. The focus was mostly on my love life or lack thereof.

For the first time, I felt a sense of pity from friends and family. They were as disappointed as I was that I was on my own and didn't have someone special to share my life experiences with.

CHAPTER 3

Overseas Travel

My life changed significantly when Aunty passed away. I was twenty-four. She had been my rock, my safety net, my dearest friend and confident. She made me breakfast in bed, taught me how to cook, and told me she loved every little hair on my head. Words cannot describe the bond we shared and the depth of love I felt for her. We shared many precious moments. And I spent hours on end listening to her words, garnering her wisdom. She shaped me.

Even to this day, I repeat her mantras over and over in my head:

- "It's a wise man that carries a coat."
- "Never trouble trouble until trouble troubles you, because you only double trouble and you trouble others too."
- "Procrastination is the thief of time."
- "Count your blessings, name them Pollyanna."
- "Don't think about the things you can't change; think about the things you can change."

And many more to draw upon.

Her passing left me broken—completely torn in two. I suffered unfathomable grief, and my world turned upside down. I began to operate on autopilot. I somehow learnt to salvage enough energy to get me through my day-to-day life and appear intact on the outside while bleeding a river of tears on the inside. Each day was painfully long. I was just going through the motions, sad, alone, and empty. It was as if I was living inside a tunnel, moving through the darkness, with no sunshine and no joy. I knew deep down that time would heal my wounds. One day, I would be happy again. One day, I would grow back my right arm and leg and everything else that felt missing. I just needed time to travel through the tunnel and find the light at the end. But I had no idea how long that would take.

After months of sorrow, I needed a distraction. I decided to try and fill my life with *stuff* to occupy my time and make the journey less painful.

Time to Escape

Judy had recently returned home after a couple of years abroad, brandishing her future husband. I listened for hours to stories of their epic adventures, some so obscure they were hardly believable. Having never possessed a passport, I found it all so surreal. The stories inspired me, and a spark was ignited. I wanted to have similar exciting life experiences.

I felt lucky to have started my career in a small city on the outskirts of Canberra. The city folk were friendly, and I especially enjoyed my morning stroll across the river each day. In winter, layered with coat, scarf, beanie, and gloves, I would step precariously over the icy grass, then make my way across the swinging timber suspension bridge, lingering midway to watch the ducks below. Sometimes I would throw them breadcrumbs and watch them scramble as they quacked like crazy. I was living in my recently purchased apartment, my home, which I was proudly painting and decorating.

Travelling overseas wasn't on my agenda. I assumed I would venture out of Australia one day, but travel abroad was something I wanted to share with my soulmate. I believed such a significant life experience should be undertaken with the man I would spend the rest of my life with, so we could create memories together. I was waiting for *the one*.

Losing my aunt shifted my focus and swayed me to rethink my point of view. I needed an escape. I needed to find some fun. It was time to be brave and venture out on my own. I couldn't wait for my soulmate any longer, and I couldn't sit on the couch alone each night feeling sorry for myself. It was time to travel.

Afraid of the unknown and petrified of going solo, I asked around if anyone had any upcoming travel plans. To my delight, a friend of a friend, a single gal about my age, was looking to go on a holiday. Perfect! We met up for hot chocolate and planned an eight-day Contiki tour of New Zealand.

After just a few short hours on a plane and the first-ever stamp in my new passport, I arrived in Christchurch, New Zealand. Immediately, I was thrown into a mix of travellers from different countries and all walks of life. For the first time in months, I was having fun—proper fun.

For eight whole days, everything was new: new people, new places, new scenery, new sounds, new smells, and new tastes. Helicopter flights, white-water rafting, speedboating, and burgeoning friendships filled my days. Best of all, I discovered that the organised adventure-tour style of travel was incredibly easy as a solo traveller. I had opened a new life chapter.

Proud of my courage to plunge into overseas travel without a significant other, I sat on the plane home contemplating my future. I felt confident I could travel further afield on my own. The adventure-tour package was a smart choice. It felt safe. I had a fun-packed itinerary and a whole load of people to share the experience with. All I had to do was turn up. I was hooked.

Fed up with hanging out with couples, upon returning home, I quit my job, packed up my home, and booked my round-the-world ticket for a year-long adventure. Everything was organised: my visas, my flights, my vaccinations, and a string of camping tours along the west coast of America and across Canada. The plan was to wind up in England, get a casual job, and figure the rest out later.

My head was buzzing with excitement and anticipation as I drove four hours north to stay with my brother for three weeks before my departure. No sooner had I arrived than a disaster happened that jolted my plans. I was out celebrating my newfound freedom and imminent departure with my brother and his friends one evening when out of the blue, I was swept off my feet by a plausible potential. How was that for bad timing?

Jim was sweet, and it wasn't the first time we had met. I knew him from my school years, and wow, had he transformed. He was now a handsomely rugged, witty man with strong arms and a muscly physique. I was impressed.

After ten days of accelerated dating, Jim and I opted to stay in touch. I really did like him. And then my plane departed.

In an era when FaceTime was not a thing (in fact, smartphones didn't even exist), I proceeded to send Jim handwritten letters, which I posted via a letterbox. How novel! On rare occasions, I was lucky enough to hear his voice for a mere few minutes as I fumbled coin after coin into the public telephone slot.

Nevertheless, I was loving my trip. I was enjoying the new people, the different cultures, and the diverse scenery. It was precisely what I needed. I had escaped. But my unwillingness to let go of the possibility of Jim changed my original focus. I was now reluctant to settle down in England for an extended period of time.

Adventure tours had added benefits. I wasn't the only solo traveller navigating the globe, and by the time I landed in London, I had collected plenty of mates to look up and hang out with. London was unlike anything I could ever have imagined: low-rise sandstone buildings, red double-decker buses, black cabs, and Beefeaters standing proud. Royalty and history were everywhere around me. I was in awe.

My school friend Jillian was living in Scotland, and I couldn't wait to see her. Jillian and I were close. Together with Maxine, Judy, and another friend, Sally, we had celebrated the end of high school on the Gold Coast in Queensland, a renowned custom known as schoolies week. Six years later, here I was sitting in her living room in Edinburgh. She soon introduced me to her Scottish life and escorted me on a driving tour around the country. I was proud of Jillian for her courage to build a new life on the other side of the world, all on her own.

Using London as a base, I explored the continent—of course, doing more adventure tours. By this time, a close friend from university, Ben, was working in London. I now had a new playmate.

I sent more letters to Jim and took a four-week trip around Western Europe, and then my brother hopped on a plane and joined me for a couple of months. My brother—or Bro, as I often call him— is shy, quirky, and stubborn, especially with me. It was nice to finally have someone permanent to share my memories with.

On a weekend getaway, Bro, Ben, and I took a short flight to Paris and stayed in a city hostel. We managed to tick off a list of must-do attractions and soak up French culture. On a budget, we ventured into the local grocery store to purchase ingredients to cook our evening meal and were surprised to learn that the purpose of our shopping basket was not to carry food; it appeared we were the only customers in the store without a pet dog in their basket. It was then that we understood the magnitude of this pet-loving culture. Carefully stepping over the doggy doo on the footpaths, we explored the museums and monuments. It was a hilarious adventure.

Together, Bro and I explored England and Egypt before taking the overnight bus back up to Scotland. It was time, however, to start making our way back home.

Did I mention my brother can be difficult? I love him dearly, but sharing a two-man tent with him for five weeks through Africa on our way back to Oz was painful. Each morning, in his cunning effort to be alone, he would excrete copious amounts of methane gas and then laugh uncontrollably at his efforts, until I eventually surrendered my position in the tent. An interesting way to bond and undoubtedly unforgettable. Africa, for its part, was truly magnificent.

Homebound

After seven months, twelve countries, forty-nine letters to Jim, and a myriad of lifelong memories, I flew home. I was hoping I could pick up my blossoming relationship where I'd left it. As I landed at Sydney airport, my chest was tight and my heart was pounding. Nervously, I held my breath as I stepped into the arrival hall. And there waiting with my mum and some of Bro's friends was Jim. He looked just as handsome as I remembered. We hugged each other close as I handed him his promised fiftieth letter.

Over the next two months, we tried hard to reignite our spark. Slowly but surely, though, we both realised we didn't have the same aspirations, and our lives just didn't fit together. Jim declared he wanted out, and although I'd come to realise our relationship was doomed, I was devastated. We lasted less than the time I spent overseas. I'd tried my best, but alas, I was single again and back to square one.

Back in the real world, I had to focus on securing a new job and finding a home. Returning to mundane day-to-day life was onerous. While I was away, I'd encountered something new almost every minute of every day. I had grown, and I felt different. Upon my return, I expected my family and friends to be changed too. But that wasn't the case; they had been living the same existence for the past seven months. Nothing had changed for them. It was only me that was different. I had evolved. My world had expanded. I was no longer satisfied to live the same day over and over again, like *Groundhog Day*.

It was time to scribe a new life plan. I was now twenty-five, but it was all good. I still had sufficient time.

Life Plan #3

1. Find my soulmate by the age of 26
2. Fall in love
3. Be in a relationship for 1 year
4. Get engaged
5. Get married by the age of 28
6. Have my first child at 28 ¾
7. Have my second child at 29 ¾
8. Turn 30
9. Live happily ever after.

CHAPTER 4

The End of the Tunnel

Keeping my furniture in storage, I shacked up with a school friend, Lisa, until I landed back on my feet. Lisa was the ideal housemate: clean, respectful, and caring. We cohabited incredibly well together … at least for a few weeks. Then Lisa became Lisa and Rick.

Bugger! I was now living with a couple—and a fresh couple at that, the kind who can't keep their hands off each other. They existed in their own little bubble, as if they were just one person blended together. Now I got to watch exactly what I wanted but couldn't find. I felt very alone yet again.

After months of dodging the couple, avoiding the lounge room, and pretending not to notice the fondling and giggling, my situation got better. I started a new job, one for which I had to drive an hour and a half in each direction, but it didn't matter. It was a good position and a progression in my career.

It was there that I met David.

Louisa Pateman

Too Much Too Soon

David may or may not have been in a relationship when we met. I don't know. It was hard to tell. Keen to show me around the office, he was welcoming and attentive and wore a warm smile. He was very conscious of his professional image and liked to keep his personal life private.

At the outset, we met daily for lunch in a park two blocks from our office. He was intelligent and thoughtful, and I enjoyed getting to know him better. I gleaned from our conversations that he was recently single—so recently that his ex-girlfriend hadn't yet moved her belongings out of his house. Suspicious but willing to trust him, I accepted that he was a free agent.

Before I could blink an eye, we were in a relationship. A few weeks after we met, one Thursday evening, David hopped in his car and drove an hour and a half to watch me play netball. Impressed with his efforts, I rewarded him with a kiss. From that moment on, we spent every day together.

After we had been dating six weeks, my housemates decided not to renew their rental lease. Damn! I was officially homeless. The obvious and most natural solution was to move in with David. He just had to get rid of his ex-lover's furniture …

This was when I came to realise that his ex may not have *been* an ex until I arrived on the scene. Unbeknownst to me, she also worked at the same company. Suffering rejection and believing I had stolen her man, she was determined to get revenge and didn't walk away quietly. Not only did we witness her outside his home peering inside with binoculars, but I also had to deflect rumours that could have tarnished my professional image.

Although scary at times, her antics didn't affect our relationship. Ironically, it made us stronger, and we went on to spend the next eighteen months together. It was comfortable living with David, who was a perfectionist, a clean freak, and a decent cook. His small two-bedroom unit was sparsely furnished and had views of the Sydney Harbour Bridge. Best of all, my journey to work was reduced to a measly twenty minutes.

Our relationship was nice—not ideal, but certainly nice. Our close friendship pushed us along, but there was a significant lack of intimacy. Over and over again, I kept asking myself: *Do I want to spend the rest of my life celibate? Do I want to pull up stumps and never explore my sexual being?* I was only twenty-six. Repeated advances to no avail left me feeling unwanted. It was a massive sacrifice to make. We had other trivial issues, just like any other couple, but was forfeiting intimacy a barrier too high to climb?

In hindsight, we acted in haste and moved in together way too soon. We opened a joint bank account and purchased an investment property without taking the time to ascertain whether the relationship was what each of us wanted or if it could go the distance.

Honoured to be Judy's bridesmaid, I watched her walk down the aisle with a man she was madly in love with. Other school friends were also getting married. I wanted my relationship with David to work. He was very dependable, and I enjoyed having a partner to attend big celebrations with. But could I give up the closeness that can only be achieved through physical intimacy?

It was at this stage that other failings surfaced, and I came to realise that I might have been sold a lemon. In the early days of our relationship, David eagerly agreed that he, too, shared my love of overseas travel. I do believe his convictions were genuine in the beginning. However, when the opportunity presented itself, he was adamant that he did not want to leave the country. Looking back, I can only assume he tried the travel idea on for size and it sounded okay, so he convinced himself he would find the urge at a later stage.

After all, he did need to convince me we were compatible to win me over. But the urge never surfaced.

There was no way I would ever be hopping on a jet plane with David by my side. Being rather possessive (he was not impressed with me spending one night away from him to catch up with my girlfriends), a solo overseas trip was never going to be on the cards.

After weighing up the pros and cons, I ended the relationship.

I was now single again at twenty-six, and I had exhausted my allocation of three introductions. Future potentials would not be meeting my extended family.

Surprisingly, it wasn't difficult cutting ties with David. After taking half of the sale proceeds from our investment property, I purchased a two-bedroom apartment in Sydney's Northern Beaches, a twelve-minute walk to the beach and an eight-minute walk to the express bus into the city. I needed a new home, and there was one thing for sure: I certainly wasn't going to live with a couple ever again. I was not in favour of self-inflicted torture. No more couples; never, ever, again!

Life Plan Revision

It was time to rethink my life plan. At twenty-six, I needed to give it a squeeze to accomplish my goals.

In revising the plan, I was forced to reconsider my priorities. I couldn't fit everything in before the cut-off date of thirty—before I turned old. I did really want children, but I acknowledged I had a lot of living to do before motherhood. I was enjoying work, and my career was progressing well. And I loved overseas travel, which I now had a passion for doing more of. I just didn't feel a burning desire for children on the near horizon. I wanted kids eventually and didn't want to miss out on having them, but they could come later.

What I really wanted was my soulmate to share my life experiences with. I kept remembering Aunty's message: get married young and grow together. I was accomplishing many goals on my own, and I was very proud of myself, but I wanted to be experiencing my life milestones with someone special. There were so many things I wanted to explore and attain, and I wanted to share those memories with the right man, *the one.*

Accepting that motherhood could be postponed, I rearranged my life plan. In doing so, I bought myself some time. My deadline of thirty now only applied to finding and securing the man of my dreams. Everything would be okay.

Life Plan #4

1. Find and fall in love with my soulmate by the age of 28
2. Be in a relationship for 1 year before getting engaged
3. Get married before turning 30
4. Have my first child at 32
5. Have my second child at 34
6. Be settled in a family home with husband and children all before turning 35
7. Live happily ever after.

I moved into my beachside apartment, single and optimistic about the future. I was happy and felt a warm sense of home. Enthusiastically, I welcomed my next chapter. Finally, I had reached the end of the tunnel.

CHAPTER 5

Unlucky in Love

Despite my impending deadline of thirty, I couldn't bring myself to settle for the wrong man. I wanted my soulmate, not just any random. This was the rest of my life I was gambling with, so I needed to get it right. The man and the relationship both had to fit. In the absence of a proven checklist from my elder matriarchs, or at least a decent explanation of how I would know when I had met *the one*, I had to rely on my own judgement. My head and my heart needed to agree; they needed to be in unison.

I began to prepare my own list. Putting pen to paper, I started writing about what I wanted in a partner, what qualities I believed my soulmate would possess, and what I wanted in a relationship. My logical brain felt this was a necessary process, but I was torn. Having a checklist seemed cold, emotionless, and somewhat counterintuitive to serendipity. It was an additional layer of analysis that didn't match up with the romantic notion of meeting someone by chance. It implied an underlying interview process with thresholds. Inevitably, the sentiment that you love someone for who he is and not who you want him to be is lost. I couldn't help but remember my late aunt telling me to fall in love first and then figure the rest out together.

The checklist was clinical and gave precedence to my head's decision, not my heart's. But having the list meant that any prospect had to prove himself to be Mr. Right. It gave me some control over my destiny.

First and foremost, I decided my soulmate needed to be a good person—a truly honourable man, one who did the right thing when presented with conflict and did not succumb to peer pressure. He would stand up for his convictions and not be afraid to speak out if needed. I wasn't sure exactly what this quality looked like; I just believed I would know it if I saw it. I also wanted someone intelligent, not necessarily book-smart but knowledgeable enough to enjoy complex conversations and hold his own in the odd debate.

Amongst a tally of other prerequisites, I especially wanted someone with a lovely, warm, captivating smile.

Ready to Get Cracking

Armed with my updated life plan and my documented checklist, I forged ahead. Living near the beach was fabulous. A short walk to the sand became an almost daily routine. I enjoyed the salt air, observed the locals, and cleared my head. The beach was my happy place.

My commute to work had increased to an hour and a half each way, but that didn't last long. I was offered a new job in the heart of Sydney, a comfortable one-hour bus ride away. No more driving in peak-hour traffic. With my career advancement and a whole new batch of co-workers, I had a new lease on life.

My newfound enthusiasm extended into my dating life. A few months into my new role, I began casually dating an old work colleague called Liam. I say *old* as in a colleague whom I had met previously in my career, not old by age. It took me by surprise when Liam asked me out. After a few informal dinner dates, I invited him to join my friends and me at social gatherings. Our time together was always light-hearted and carefree.

It was a strange time for me, as until now, I had only ever been in a committed relationship or single. I had never ventured into the casual dating scene, and I didn't know the rules. I assumed Liam and I weren't exclusive, although we hadn't had the discussion. It just never came up.

Liam accompanied my friends and I on a camping trip, and we partook in a couple of overnight stays at each other's houses. From the outside, it looked like the beginnings of a real relationship, but weirdly, we were never physically intimate. When we slept together, we actually just slept. The bedsheets wrapped around my body and folded down to the centre of the bed before covering Liam, creating a physical divide between us. Those centimetres of dead space may as well have been as big as the Grand Canyon. I couldn't have felt further away. No spooning, no affection, no physical touch. It was like sharing a bed with my brother. Even my girlfriends got closer to me when sharing a bed. After failing to surpass the platonic stage, the casual dates went no further.

All good, I hadn't wasted too much time.

Still single, I dove into work and thoroughly enjoyed my new home and new surroundings. Judy and Maxine lived nearly two hours away, so I needed to reinvent my social life. Judy was now married, as were most of my other girlfriends, so once a month I would venture north to spend the weekend hanging out with couples. Once a month was enough to remind me that I felt awkward and left out and that I was failing my life plan. I loved catching up with the girls and keeping connected, but spending time with them and their husbands reminded me I was lonely. It was just highlighting what I didn't have.

Not Enough Questions

I started spending more time at work. I also started spending more time with a colleague called Hugh. Hugh and I joined the organisation around the same time in our respective roles and were thrown together to learn the ropes. We got on extremely well, and I was keen to find out more about him.

I have been told by many that I am a talkative person. I was once described as being able to talk underwater with a mouthful of marbles. I'm not so sure, but I am indeed blessed with the gift of the gab. Suffice to say, sometimes my conversations with Hugh would lead well into the evening, so together, we would venture out of the office to grab some dinner. The more time I spent with him, the more attractive he became. Hugh was cheeky and fun, intelligent and interesting. He delighted in tormenting me, and by any definition, flirted with me. Of course, I flirted back.

To my understanding, he was single. From the information I gleaned during our lengthy discussions of our love lives, he had just come out of a relationship with a Scottish girl whom he had met on holidays. Her name was Annabel. They had met and fallen in love on a whirlwind overseas holiday, and she had proceeded to follow him on his extended travels. Time passed, and then Annabel made a significant effort to spend Christmas with Hugh and his family in Australia. My recollection of our conversations led me to believe that he still had feelings for Annabel but was not convinced she was the one, and there was no further arrangement to see her again.

Okay, so he had some unresolved feelings, but he *was* apparently single. That was enough information to give me hope. I decided I wanted him. He ticked every box on my checklist, and my heart was in. I was utterly smitten. I was almost in love. This was it. I was going to get my happily-ever-after. Never mind that I wasn't even in a relationship with him; that was just a trivial detail.

Having now decided Hugh was the one, I didn't hold back with my flirting, and I stole whatever time I could get with him in and out of the office. We continued to talk about his feelings for Annabel, and I knew he wasn't ready for a new relationship. For the time being, I was content just to be in his company. When we were together, we laughed so hard we cried. We bounced off each other and shared common interests.

And then one night it happened: we had an accident. And by *accident*, I mean the unplanned kind that occurs in the heat of the moment. A threshold had been crossed, a boundary had been broken, and we finally reached home base. It was fun, exciting, and spontaneous. Months of flirting and anticipation had come to fruition.

The way it happened was not glamorous, but it happened nonetheless. I drove home that night on a massive high. I was hopeful that this would have enough of an impact to rattle his feelings for Annabel—that he would give me a chance. I smiled and dreamt happy dreams.

When I walked into work the next morning, I felt secretly smug, like a little girl. Hugh sat only a few desks away from me, and I couldn't wait to see him. I was nervous that our co-workers would guess what was going on from the smile on my face. I'm not very good at hiding my feelings. In fact, I'm atrocious at it. I never did manage to master that skill.

By morning tea, we had found an excuse to head out of the office for a site inspection. We drove about twenty minutes to the site chatting about nothing, and then he dropped a bombshell.

He began by saying, "I had fun last night, and I don't want to upset you, but ..."

My heart started racing. What was he about to say? I felt panicked.

"But," he said again, "I haven't been completely honest with you."

I could hardly breathe. I sat stiff, holding the edge of my seat, bracing myself for what was about to come out of his mouth.

"I still have feelings for Kristin," he confessed.

What the fuck? Who the heck was Kristin? Where did *this* woman come from? Did he just say the wrong woman's name? I sat motionless. I must have looked stunned as he went on to explain the situation without me uttering a word. I barely moved a muscle. He had rendered me speechless.

Kristin, I now learned, was Hugh's girlfriend before Annabel. The plot just kept getting thicker. All the time he had been talking about Annabel and his unresolved feelings for his Scottish love, he had neglected to tell me about Kristin. Was this guy for real?

He went on to explain that Annabel was kind of a rebound relationship after Kristin had abruptly broken up with him, and his trip overseas was his escape. But now Kristin had had a change of heart and wanted him back. Not only did she want him back, but she also wanted to settle down and marry him, and he was genuinely considering her offer. Whoa! Talk about being blindsided.

This information was like a bullet through my heart. How could I not have known about this? I had spent hours and hours and hours on end talking to him over the past few months. After endless conversations and workshopping about his feelings for Annabel, how could the issue of Kristin not have been thrown into the discussion?

I didn't know how to respond. I was gutted, shell-shocked, and without words. I was now competing with not one woman for Hugh's affection but two. I put on a brave face for the remainder of the car trip. I wanted to cry, but my pride took over.

The news didn't change how I felt about Hugh, although it should have. I was too invested. I should have walked away in disgust at the deception. Instead, I rationalised that he didn't really lie to me, he just chose to omit some crucial information—information that would have been nice to have before the accident.

Alas, I empathised about how difficult this must have been for him, and foolishly, I stuck around. Not only did I continue to spend regular time with him, I now found myself talking through his unclear feelings for Annabel *and* Kristin. I gave him my shoulder to lean on while he debated his dilemma and decided which girl to choose. Annabel lived overseas, and they hadn't spent enough time together for him to know if what they had would last. Kristin was the least risky, as he had spent the most time with her, and he had previously lived with her.

Kristin was the one who got away after she jilted him, and Annabel was the rebound. So what was I? Just someone to flirt with and take his mind off his impending decision? Hugh described Kristin as being pretty, very quiet, and from what I could gather, also very boring. She was safe and homely. She was wife material. Annabel, on the other hand, was chirpy and had an adorable accent.

And where did I stand in this mix? I was clearly third. Hugh described me as "too much fun." I wasn't what he imagined a wife to be. I didn't have the runs on the board, and I wasn't tame enough. He didn't consider me a safe bet. So there I had it: I was never going to be Mrs. Hugh.

I hung onto hope for a few more months, spending more time with him and having more accidents. Deep down, I desperately wanted him to see how good we were together and that he needed to ditch the other two and choose me. How could he not see we would have had the most amazing life together? After six months of this saga, my pride and sanity finally took over. My head stepped in to instruct my heart that enough was enough. I was a victim of self-inflicted torture. No woman should have to sit back and entertain the man she loves while he pines over two other women. That was not okay! I was worth more than this.

With enormous pain and heartache, I had to stop spending time with Hugh and stop allowing him to use me as his sounding board for his problems. Sad and hurt, I walked away and retreated to the company of my girlfriends.

Still Not Enough Questions

Over the next few months, I focused on work and tried to forget my relationship woes. I decided to take a ten-day holiday to Thailand to escape my heartache. As was becoming my signature travel, I joined an organised adventure tour, again as a solo traveller.

Refocused and back on track, I was lucky to be moved to a different office location. The organisation, currently based in Sydney's central business district with around two hundred staff across a spectrum of internal working divisions, was now splitting up into smaller site offices across greater Sydney. A handful of us were relocating west, less than twenty minutes from the city by car—a close-knit friendly group with no Hugh!

The age profile of the organisation was skewed towards lots of enthusiastic young staff. And by *young*, I mean twenties and thirties. Most of the people were sociable, and my role allowed me to cross paths with a multitude of new faces.

One such face belonged to a man called Dan. Dan was polite, well-dressed, and not bad on the eyes. He was probably a few years older than me. Our respective roles required us to catch up from time to time to progress work matters. Before my office relocation, Dan had started to stop by my desk on a more regular basis. I assumed he was chasing up outstanding work issues before I headed out to site.

Comfortably settled into my new office, I received a phone call from Dan as I was about to head home one afternoon. The conversation started with five minutes of work discussion and then moved on to chatter about our personal lives. I don't recall being the one to initiate the more personal questions, but being one to never say no to a conversation, I was happy to chat.

About an hour into the phone call, he made a point of telling me his living arrangements. Now, I may not remember the exact words, but I certainly remember the gist of what was said: "I'm bacheloring it at the moment."

He then proceeded to invite me over for dinner—as in dinner right then, that night, at his house. It was not a request for a date on the upcoming weekend. No. It was a midweek spur-of-the-moment invitation. I was taken aback at first, but the request didn't offend me, and I was surprisingly flattered. After maybe five minutes of contemplation, I thought, *Why not? He seems like a sweet guy. What harm could a midweek dinner date do?*

I finished work, hopped in my car, purchased a bottle of wine, and presented myself at Dan's apartment. He cooked me a meal that must have been good, although I don't recall the detail. What I do remember was that his apartment was very clean and tidy, with everything colour-coordinated—white with splashes of green ornaments and scatter cushions. I was impressed. We babbled on for hours, and I went on my merry way.

Over the following four weeks, Dan and I spent considerable time together, almost daily, catching up for lunches or coffees and, unsurprisingly, the occasional intimate sleepover. We even attended a social work function together. We didn't hold hands or show affection, but we had only been dating a couple of weeks, so it would definitely not be appropriate to be displaying affection amongst our comrades.

Four and a half weeks into our whirlwind encounter, I noticed a change. I say *encounter*, as I was still nursing my recent rejection, and I wasn't about to throw my heart out to get slaughtered. The courtship was nevertheless proving itself to be lots of fun.

I turned up at Dan's apartment for another home-cooked meal. This time, however, something was awry. The mood was different; Dan's demeanour was different. I wandered into the kitchen, where he was preparing our meal, and noticed on the benchtop a group of cookbooks. The upright books were divided into two sections, and between them was a photo of a woman. Very strange … I had never seen this photo before.

I walked back out to the dining room, and there on the sideboard stood another picture of this same woman. My heart began to race. What the heck was going on? Why were there photographs of this woman strategically placed around his home?

As we sat down to eat, I started to look carefully around the room. Dan's apartment really was immaculately colour-coordinated; the decor was perfectly matched. Our conversation, unlike at previous dinners, was stifled and uncomfortable. And then it dawned on me that we had never had a lengthy discussion about our respective relationship statuses. During our phone call the night of our first dinner date, I had declared my single standing, and I had assumed Dan's confessed bachelor status meant that he was single too. Why else would he invite me over for dinner and then proceed to spend almost every day with me?

The photograph required immediate clarification, so I asked, "Dan, are you single?"

He turned and gave me a defeated look, his face awkwardly distorted, followed by an uncomfortable reply: "No."

What? Did he just say *no*? Aghast, I tried to hold myself together. My heart was on fire, and my palms began to sweat. Taking a deep breath, I calmly asked, "What do you mean?"

To which he replied, "I'm seeing someone."

Okay. A touch of relief. I could deal with "seeing someone." To me, that signified a casual dating situation, one where you might or might not be exclusive. It was certainly not ideal, but I guess I could forgive the neglected information.

To avoid any confusion, I needed further explanation. "So, do you mean you're casually dating someone?" I naively asked.

To which he responded, "No. We live together."

What the heck! My mouth fell completely open with shock. I was sitting in another woman's house, having slept with her partner. The term *repulsion* was an understatement.

I was halfway through my meal when this information was revealed. I had to swallow my food. I had to stay calm. I had to get the hell out of there! I don't even know why I felt obligated to finish my meal. I think it was pride. My pride was telling me, *Don't react. Don't give him the satisfaction of showing sorrow.* Although it wasn't sadness I was feeling.

My senses were in overdrive, and I was questioning all my character-assessment capabilities. How did I not see this coming? Why had I not asked more questions? Why had I assumed he was a good person without even a partial interrogation? I felt violated. I felt like I had just found out I was having dinner with Ted Bundy.

While gulping down the food in front of me, I asked, "Where is she?"

That's when I found out that Antonella, his partner of several years, was visiting her family in Columbia and due to come home from her five-week trip within the next couple of days. The timeline was absurd. He had literally dropped Antonella off at the airport the very same day he invited me over for dinner. Wow, was he slick! And now it was time to dispose of me, as she was on a plane homeward bound.

I politely excused myself and drove home, my head filled with complete disbelief.

The following days at work, I regained my composure and digested the events of the past month. Clearly, I had not asked enough questions. I was willing to plough head first into a romantic liaison with a man I hardly knew. I had assumed he was open and honest and that his intentions were honourable. I assumed he was a decent man. His work persona suggested he was respectable and a gentleman. Obviously, I made too many assumptions.

Lesson learnt: get clarification on the definition of relationship status terms before turning up at a man's house. In this instance, the term *bacheloring* did not equal living alone. Dan had barely been on his own for a couple of hours at the most! And "seeing someone" did not equal casual dating. On the contrary, Dan's definition was a girlfriend of many years. My take-home from this encounter was distrust and deception. Be more aware!

A few weeks later, my self-esteem was in check, and I was back in control. Returning to my old office in the city for a team meeting, I took the lift alone to the fifth level. The doors opened at level two, and there stood Dan. Oh, how the universe is amusing sometimes! He looked at me like a little boy scolded and asked, "Should I take another lift?"

I laughed. "No, hop in. I won't bite," I teased.

After the meeting, Dan joined me for coffee. It was nice to see him remorseful for what he had done. I wanted to convince myself that my judgement of character was not diabolically wrong. We talked about the series of events, and I asked him why he pursued me. His response, although completely amiss, appeared to come from the right place. He admitted he had admired me for a long time and always looked for ways to stop by my desk when I was working in the city office. He simply enjoyed my company. So, when the opportunity presented itself to spend alone time with me, he didn't hold back. Perhaps I shouldn't have been so willing.

He talked about his tormented relationship with Antonella, detailing their problems, his doubts, and his desire to leave her on several occasions. He sold me his sob story. I appreciated that half of what he told me was glorification to make himself look better and validate his actions, but it worked. I began to feel sorry for him. I saw him as a man trapped in an unhappy relationship who wanted something better but couldn't bring himself to get out.

I interrogated him as to why he didn't simply tell Antonella not to come home or break up with her upon her return. It was evident he didn't have the courage to be single—or at least risk being single if things didn't work out with me.

A wave of bravado swept over me. Dan was afraid to be single—so afraid, he was willing to forego any chance of genuine happiness. I was incredibly relieved when I realised I didn't share his fear. I couldn't imagine choosing to stay in an unfulfilling relationship with someone who wasn't *the one*. My perspective immediately changed. For the first time in my life, I was grateful for my failed relationships. I was thankful I was free to find a good man and a good relationship and not stay trapped by fear.

Dan's misfortune left me feeling empowered. My Dan saga turned out to be a life lesson highlighting what happens when you settle for the wrong person, fail to possess the courage to be single, and thus are unable to go forth and create the best life possible.

CHAPTER 6

New Adventures Abroad

Another year down and another significant career achievement. My work contract was coming to an end. I was a couple of months shy of twenty-eight and still single.

As a reward to myself, I embarked on a three-week journey to Peru and Bolivia, sailing on Lake Titicaca in a reed boat, staying with a local family in a mud-brick two-room house with an outside kitchen and long-drop toilet, and hiking the Inca Trail. The four days trekking the forty kilometres to Machu Picchu, the lost city of the Incas, was truly cathartic. Through mystic mountains, up and over Dead Woman's Pass, I slowly but surely put one foot in front of the other while porters sped past carrying backpacks bigger than a body. I was able to spend many hours reassessing my life, reminiscing, and reflecting, while making new friends along the way.

Upon returning home, I decided I needed a work challenge—something that would push me outside my comfort zone. I had forged a friendship with a lovely New Zealand couple on my adventure. They were living in London, undertaking their overseas experience, their "OE," as they described it. And they inspired me to do the same. They had planted a seed. I needed to find work abroad.

It took me four months to sow the seed. Without family ties to the motherland, I needed to land a job with a company that would sponsor my employment, arrange a work visa, and relocate my belongings. Word of mouth, some work in kind, and sufficient negotiation skills landed me in Guildford, in the county of Surrey, with a two-year work contract.

It was 2001. I was twenty-eight, single, and looking forward to this next chapter.

Grateful for Girlfriends

I immersed myself in English life. I was thankful for my Kiwi friends who had inspired my journey to the other side of the world, but they lived in London, and visiting them was almost a two-hour round trip. Over time, our catch-ups became less frequent.

I was fortunate Jillian was still living in the British Isles. Having met and married an Englishman, she was now settled in a small township near Leeds. Once a month, I would drive four hours north to spend the weekend with her, and on occasion, she would head south to visit me. I gathered a few other friends, but as was the case back home, they were all couples. On the other side of the globe, I was once again feeling very single and very alone.

Fortuitously, about four months into my overseas experience, Zoe, another friend from home, packed up her belongings and moved to nearby Godalming, a picturesque little village in Surrey. Our friendship had had a rocky beginning. She was the sister of Ross, my boyfriend who wanted to "experience other women." Whilst dating Ross, I was convinced Zoe didn't approve of me. Perhaps this belief came about after she mentioned in passing that she'd expected her brother to choose a girlfriend who didn't come from a broken family.

At the time, her comment hit a raw nerve. Devastated that I didn't live up to her standards, and reminded of the fact that I didn't have the perfect Mum and Dad I'd longed for as a child, I spent hours crying in the arms of my aunt while she tried to convince me I was worthy of being loved.

Strangely, though, Zoe and I now got on like a house on fire. Intelligent, insightful, and possessing infectious energy, she had a knack for making me question myself, forcing me to see different perspectives. Post-break-up with Ross, my friendship with Zoe went from strength to strength. Very quickly, she developed a better understanding of me than I had of myself at times.

A year younger than me, she was also single. With her arrival in Surrey, I now had a familiar face from home and a friend with whom to explore Great Britain. I was no longer alone and no longer the third wheel. Life had just become a thousand times better.

We spent many weekends exploring, making day trips to Brighton pier and the pebbly coastline of Sussex, having hot lunches in cozy English pubs, and taking long drives through the rolling green countryside. We mostly travelled in my small unreliable five-door 1984 hatchback I had purchased second-hand to get me to and from work. We once had to sleep in that hatchback on a trip to Wales when our bright idea of hopping in the car on a bank holiday weekend and driving as far west as we could muster without booking accommodation in advance, led to one of our most memorable adventures.

In the middle of Wales, six hours from home, with not a single vacant room within reach, we found ourselves parked at a roadside stopping bay, pulled up for the night. No toilet, no street lighting, no shower. We detoured to a pub and indulged in a hearty hot meal before retreating to sleep uncomfortably squashed up in my little car. With the front seats tilted back as far as the knob would turn, our legs bent and wedged under the steering wheel or dashboard, and our spare clothing folded under our heads as makeshift pillows, we tried to sleep, though we were freezing out there in the dark. Alert and on edge, we jumped at every sound. With the doors locked, I left the keys in the ignition for an emergency start if we needed to act in haste. We lived to tell the story, but it was the last time we failed to book accommodation in advance.

Zoe and I can both talk until the cows come home. During our time in England, and beyond, we spent hours and hours deliberating over anything and everything. We especially enjoyed talking about our potential love interests and secret crushes. Together we attempted to interpret the actions and intentions of the opposite sex, often getting it completely wrong. We gave each other advice and feedback in the arena of love, albeit often misguided and misconstrued. It was a case of the blind leading the blind. We laughed and smiled, and our friendship grew.

Losing the Plot

Half a year into my overseas experience, I developed a crush on one of my flatmates. I was living in a share house in Guildford with five young adults, all single and from different walks of life. I wasn't used to the shared-house set-up. At home, I had lived on my own, or with a romantic partner, or with only one flatmate (except the one instance of living with a couple, but let's not remember that torture). Living in a house with four other people and only one combined bathroom and toilet proved to be challenging.

Life was on a schedule. I had to patiently wait to use the small alley-style kitchen with my one designated storage cupboard. I had to limit my time in the one common living room, which was only big enough to seat four people comfortably, and I had to adhere to the roster for the morning toilet and shower.

We shared the same roof, but we seldom shared the same company. When all five housemates got together, we would laugh over our own versions of the English language. An American, a Dutch, an Australian, and two Brits (one from the north of England and one from the south), we all had different words to describe the same thing. Was I sleeping under a duvet, a doona, or a comforter? And was my car a lemon, a banger, or a jalopy? Was I taking a bath or a barrrth, pronouncing the *r* or not?

After a few months of cheeky smiles, I took a fancy to my fellow northern Englishman. Our conversations became flirtatious, and we started taking extra interest in each other's movements. His name was Trent. Shortly after, we hooked up. We became very comfortable very quickly. Then, as fast as the relationship had started, it ended. And it ended disastrously.

I'm guessing we lasted three months, perhaps more; I don't particularly remember. What I do remember is how badly I behaved when we broke up. I clearly lost the plot.

By now, I was getting close to twenty-nine. I had endured a couple of unrequited crushes, and my life plan was looking grim. Trent was a beacon of hope. I was excited, my intentions were genuine, and I had grand expectations. It just so happened Trent didn't have the same vision … well, at least not with me. When he told me he thought we should just be friends, he admitted he had met someone else, and there was clearly an overlap. I should have been appreciative that he was open and honest, but I couldn't get past the glaring issue of the overlap. An *overlap*! In my eyes this constituted cheating.

In my version of reality, we were spending every night together in an exclusive relationship. Perhaps not every night, given he had the time to undertake an overlap. Did I fail to communicate my understanding that we were, in fact, in a solid, steady relationship? None of that mattered. Trent had already moved on, and now his new girlfriend was spending every night at our house. Talk about uncomfortable!

Maybe it was the pressure and disappointment of seeing my life plan slip away, or perhaps it was my severely damaged pride that led to my behaviour. It was likely a culmination of many factors, but in a nutshell, I behaved in a manner that was unbecoming and embarrassing. I spat the dummy (pacifier for the non-Australians) and carried on like a pork chop. There were accusations, swearing, yelling, and insults, all fired at Trent. I was shocked, I was angry, and I was making sure he knew it.

For the first time in my life, I personally lived out the saying, "Hell hath no fury like a woman scorned." I was scorned, and I wasn't walking away quietly. I behaved like a lunatic with no rationale whatsoever.

I cringe now looking back on the situation and how I mishandled it. Trent merely met someone else. And to be fair, he did have the decency to tell me about the overlap. He could have hidden it from me but chose to be open and honest. Poor guy, he probably won't ever do that again.

I was suffering from rejection, that's all—just disappointment and unrequited affection. With the benefit of hindsight, I know there was no way we were even close to being compatible as life partners. Trent just happened to realise this before me.

After a month of torturing myself and those around me, my self-respect prevailed, and I knew I needed to move out. Thankfully, the universe stepped in. I was headhunted for a job with a competing company. The new role involved not only moving to a new house but also moving to a new country. I immediately snapped up the opportunity to escape.

Age thirty was just around the corner, but I decided to take a break from my life plan. I needed to take stock of my emotions and focus on regaining my self-worth. Moving to Greece was the perfect solution.

Take-home lesson from England: don't ever date your housemates. Trent was not worth the grief or angst.

CHAPTER 7

Separated But Not Divorced

Zoe helped me pack up my belongings and waved me goodbye as I headed to Greece in my 1984 hatchback. My lovely Kiwi friend, Sandy, took a leave of absence from her boyfriend and escorted me on a week-long journey, driving across France and Italy, and then onto an overnight ship headed for Patras, Greece. Not only was I manoeuvring through a complex road network attempting to read road signs in a foreign language, but I was also driving a left-hand drive vehicle in countries that travel on the right side of the road. It was late 2001, and we didn't have the luxury of GPS or handheld navigational devices. Sandy had the road maps, and I had the steering wheel. With only one incident where I drove the wrong way around a roundabout and a brief stint using the road shoulder as a through-traffic lane in Greece (in line with the locals), I managed to get us to our destination, unscathed and with all our limbs in place. It was a fun-filled adventure to add to the many others I was experiencing.

Greece was a place like no other. I didn't have time to think about Trent or any other boys once I arrived. I was fully immersed in a new job, a new culture, a new language, and an entirely new way of life. The company set me up temporarily in an apartment in the centre of Athens, walking distance from the office. I was paired up with Victoria, a beautiful young Canadian-Greek girl who took me under her wing, acted as my interpreter, and helped me find my feet. The office was a hive of people moving about, speaking Greek, and smoking cigarettes.

I wasn't used to the smoking, and I couldn't escape it, not even in McDonald's. I detested cigarettes. In my teens, Maxine was always trying to get people to drive her to buy a packet of smokes. But she knew better than to ask me. Not only would I not drive her, but I also refused to even stop at a service station if she was in the car. In restaurants, I was that problematic patron demanding to be relocated to a better table so I didn't have to suck in remnants of putrid, stale cigarette smoke. But now I had to purse my lips. I was a guest in this country, and they all smoked like chimneys.

I also wasn't used to the late-night culinary practices. I worked with a group of English-speaking expatriates from different companies, and we would often dine together at night—*late* at night. In Greece, the restaurants would start getting busy around ten o'clock. In true Greek fashion, my midweek festivities would see me getting into bed around one in the morning. I was exhausted!

Each morning, I would get into work and watch the daily office ritual. My Greek counterparts were addicted to their morning frappé. Iced frappés were made with several heaped teaspoons of instant coffee, ice cubes, sugar, and milk, blended together and sipped through a long straw extending from a tall tumbler. The blender, aka the frappé machine, was in high demand each morning, with many tired staff members eager to get their energy boost. The next hour would see people with a frappé in one hand, cigarette in the other, one-finger typing on their computer keyboard. By mid-morning, the office was back to what I would call normal, with a rush of activity and significantly increased productivity. Learning about a different culture was incredibly fascinating. I was splitting my leisure time between the local café scene with Victoria and sport and dining with my newfound expat friends. I was grateful to be experiencing the local culture, but I couldn't speak the language, and as much as the locals tried to make me feel included by speaking English, within an hour, the conversations always reverted to Greek. I was grateful for the one hour.

My work package included paid accommodation, so I chose to move into a sea-view apartment in the trendy beachside suburb of Glyfada. On the weekends, I would walk into town along the beach, passing tanned elderly men in skimpy swimwear playing a game with racquets and a ball, laughing and having fun. The beaches in Greece, I learnt, had an unwritten status ranking. You couldn't, or shouldn't, visit just any beach. It had to be the *right* beach. Image, it seemed, was paramount.

Greece afforded me a new perspective on being single. My expat work colleagues were a mix of couples and singles, with some leaving their partners and families back in Australia. My Greek colleagues, however, would not dare to admit they were single. As was the norm, Victoria admitted that she had made an agreement with Stefanos, another work colleague, to be her pretend boyfriend. They were not a couple; they simply agreed to tell people they were an item, as this presented a higher community status than being single. It was a strange custom, one that led to some interesting conversations about my declaration of being on my own, and a reinforcement in my mind that women needed to find a man to be seen as successful.

Honking horns, double parking, and driving through red lights—I enjoyed the contrasts to home. I loved seeing the hundreds of mopeds zooming the streets; Vespas the locals called them. I saw plenty of women perched on a motorised scooter, handbag under one arm, helmet hanging off the other arm, not on their head, as that would cause helmet hair. It was the law to wear a helmet; it just didn't specify which part of the body it had to be worn on.

Greek women, in my experience, were consumed with their appearance—their make-up and their manicured locks. Well, at least the younger women were. At any time of day, I would find at least five women standing in front of the mirror in the office bathroom reapplying make-up. It was a constant fight to get to the basin, pushing my way in to wash my hands. Dozens of make-up cases lined the benchtop. To the dismay of one of my female co-workers, I didn't reapply my make-up. I only wore lipstick, and I used a brand that stayed on all day. I didn't need to primp.

I am Australian. I have fair skin and freckles. I would need to apply a truckload of foundation to cover up all my blemishes. No. I was happy with my looks. I didn't feel the need to plaster myself with a mask. Apart from the uncomfortable feeling of gunk on my face, it just wasn't me. I was casual and carefree, with a touch of lippy for good measure.

Since I had dark brown hair, locals often spoke to me in Greek, thinking I was a native. As much as I tried, I just couldn't pick up the language. I could read partial sentences, say *yes, no, please,* and *thank you.* I remember catching the bus home from work sometimes and watching people talk to each other using words I couldn't understand. Other people were interacting and connecting while I sat back as the observer, an outcast unable to contribute.

My work crowd was a mix of young and old from different walks of life. Wednesday nights, I would play social tennis with a couple I knew from Australia, and I joined a group of expat colleagues for mixed soccer (football) games. I was feeling settled. I allowed myself to relax and just embrace life. My relationship woes were far gone, and I didn't even give the life plan a thought. I felt invigorated and free. I was back to my old self.

In the office, I wasn't perturbed by the language barrier. It became the norm to hear a barrage of what sounded like cursing and fighting in meetings, only to find out it was polite Greek-style banter and raising your voice was expected.

Surprise Request

When necessary, I would retreat to my English-speaking work colleagues. I was especially drawn to Don, who was twenty years my senior. Don was witty and fun to be around. Held in high regard by his peers and considered authoritative as an architect, he was someone with whom I found myself always drifting into conversation. He made me laugh.

Don had been in Greece for several months on his own. He wore a wedding ring, but I was told he was separated, and I heard on the office grapevine that he had found himself a female companion since arriving. I wasn't too fussed about what he was or wasn't doing in his personal life; he was just my friendly workmate who I thoroughly enjoyed spending time with.

Apparently, Don also enjoyed my company—so much so that he propositioned me out of the blue one evening. We were walking in the backstreets of Athens on our way to a restaurant to meet our fellow colleagues when he turned to me and asked, "Do you want to have an affair?" Just like that, with no romantic gesture to sweep me off my feet. No. Short and straight to the point. *Do you want to have an affair?*

Had I heard him correctly? Surely it was a Freudian slip. He didn't really mean to ask me that question. For a few moments, I decided he was just joking, as he was rather playful and cheeky. It was in his character to stir the pot. But I wasn't quite sure.

And what did he mean by *affair?* Our twenty-year age gap did result in us speaking a different language sometimes. Was he asking for a one-night stand? Was he asking for a fling? I wasn't game enough to ask for an explanation.

Until that moment in time, Don had never played a part in any of my romantic fantasies, perhaps because of the age gap or possibly because of the minor detail of him wearing a wedding ring. For the next few seconds, I decided to consider his proposition seriously. I was undeniably drawn to him. I was living in a foreign country on a two-year work assignment, and I was taking a break from my life plan since it was screwing with my head. Don was fun. Don was confident. Don didn't care too much about what other people thought.

On a whim, I turned to him, shrugged my shoulders, and said, "Okay."

And that was how we got together: a very unromantic union that blossomed into a very romantic relationship.

Now would be the time to apply some perspective. Yes, Don was married on paper, but he had been living apart from his wife for almost a year. Over many conversations, I learnt he had been unfulfilled in his marriage for several years. Work became his sanctuary from an unhappy home life where he felt neglected and lonely.

I understood his legal commitment. But it didn't matter at that moment; separated was good enough. I was in Greece, and I had him all to myself. I decided this would be a fling, a holiday romance, and an escape from my life plan. In an unfamiliar country, I found it easy to live in the now. I wasn't planning on spending the rest of my life with Don. I didn't have to decipher if he was *the one*. I could just enjoy our time together. It was temporary.

From the very beginning, we spent almost every night together. We decided not to openly admit our relationship to our work colleagues, so we either spent our time alone or with Don's group of friends. In the months before my arrival, Don had extricated himself from the social work gatherings and found his own little expat community in Glyfada, close to where I lived, an hour's drive from work, and far from the prying eyes of our workmates. It was amongst this group that I made some lifelong friendships.

The Glyfada expat community became my family. We spent lots of time with Patsy, Polly, and Tim. During the week, Don and I would meet our friends after work at the Black Sheep Tavern for a hit of snooker and many hands of cards. On weekends, we would congregate at the beach or the top floor of Hotel Emintina, just a five-minute walk from my home, to laze around the pool and chat. We dined at all the local restaurants, drank wine, and enjoyed the local cuisine.

Patsy and I got on incredibly well. Blonde-haired and blue-eyed, Patsy was a stunner. Having lived in Greece for five years, she had built her own English-speaking nanny agency for elite clients. She was my age, confident and forthright, and I liked her immediately. She was one of my tribe. Living with her Greek boyfriend, Nikos, she was instrumental in organising all the social activities—the perfect planner.

As part of my employment contract, I negotiated four trips a year back to England. This allowed me to catch up with Zoe and stay connected to the land I had fallen in love with. In turn, I was blessed with visits from Zoe, her parents, and my thick-and-thin partner in crime Maxine. Jillian also flew across the Channel to spend some time with me.

Ever the perfect host, I loved showing my friends around my new country, introducing them to, among other things, the local tavernas serving the freshest seafood with a classic Greek salad. I especially loved the fried whitebait and the lightly battered calamari—real calamari, thick chunks of white flesh, no processed flawlessly round rings here. And lots of feta cheese! Oh, and did I mention the prawn saganaki? My mouth waters just thinking about it.

And of course, as host, I dutifully took my guests to the Greek islands, most with golden sand and blue waters, no waves, just calm, peaceful paradise. I adored the white and blue landscape on Mykonos, Santorini and Paros, as was typical of the Cycladic islands. The colours of the flag painted on every building, white walls with blue shutters and blue domes, and the national flag proudly flying high, patriotism was at the heart of every citizen—it was lovely to observe. And in the cafes, people would talk and drink over a friendly game of backgammon.

I was twenty-nine, I was dating a fifty-year-old, and I was having the time of my life.

I had never imagined dating someone so old. It's funny now that I think about it. Don was only fifty, and as I write this story, I am currently in my mid-forties, with fifty looming just around the corner. But at twenty-nine, dating someone fifty seemed like a huge leap. It was risky, unknown territory. My friends back home couldn't fathom the idea. They laughed it off and considered me deserving of a fling, given my failure in finding *the one* thus far.

Being with someone older had its benefits. Don introduced me to conversations and life experiences I hadn't been previously exposed to. He loved to socialise, loved the pub, loved fine dining, and loved to have a glass of wine or five or six. Together we were playful and made the most of every moment.

Keeping our relationship secret from our work colleagues was an interesting challenge. Don's apartment was closer to work than mine and close to Athens city centre. On the occasions we travelled to work by train, we would endeavour to leave the office ten minutes apart, to deflect suspicion, then meet up on the train-station platform. We wanted to keep the relationship sacred and avoid the scrutiny of judgemental work colleagues. Nonchalantly, we would stand near each other on the platform, holding the same handrail. Only our fingers would touch, and when they did, my heart rate would soar. That's when I knew I had accidentally fallen in love.

For six months solid, we were a couple our friends envied ... until Don's work contract came to an unexpected end. The honeymoon was about to be over, and reality was about to kick in. I had known this day would come. I had rationalised that our relationship had to be temporary. Yes, I would miss Don dearly, but I hoped that one day I would meet a younger man with whom I would have this much fun. It was okay. This was just a dress rehearsal for the real deal. I would be fine. Time was all I would need.

Don decided to stay an extra month in Greece with me before heading back to Australia. We took the opportunity to travel to more islands, snorkel, fish, and relax by the breathtaking Mediterranean Sea. During this month, I kept telling myself I needed to have as much fun as possible before it all came to an end. I tried to treat it like the holiday fling it was intended to be, distance myself emotionally, and prepare for the next chapter.

As we drew closer to separation day, we were in my apartment one morning when Don turned to me and asked, "Do you think we have a chance?"

My breath quickened, and my heart started pounding. It was a valid question, one requiring a lot of discussion. I was excited by the prospect and did a little dance inside my head, but I needed to be sure it could work.

Don was technically married, with teenage children back in Australia, and I was twenty-nine, wanting to get married and have

59

my own children. Did our relationship have any real chance of survival? We had been tucked away in our own little bubble with complete focus on one another. Would we be able to withstand a bombardment of external distractions?

We dearly loved each other, and it made sense to build a future together. We just needed to figure out how. I decided I needed to give us a chance. So it was agreed: Don would head back to Australia, officially end his marriage, and find a house for the two of us to move into, and I would quit my job in Greece, relocate back to Oz, and move into our new home. It was a six-week plan, and there was no time to waste.

In coming to the decision to give us a go, Don agreed to father one more child with me. Just one. But he knew I was only twenty-nine and needed to realise my life dream of becoming a mum.

Thus, it was set. It was really happening. Ironically, when I wasn't looking for my soulmate, it appeared I had found him.

With a touch of sadness and an enormous amount of anticipation, I waved goodbye to Don, quit my job, and started to pack up my life in Greece. It was time to start the rest of my life.

Homecoming

Saying goodbye to my Glyfada friends was hard, but the timing was right. My closest friends were starting to make their own plans to leave Greece for greener pastures, so my departure was on cue. Patsy and Nikos were moving to New Zealand, and I was hoping I would cross paths with them again.

On the plane back to Australia, I started to feel trepidation. What if it didn't work? Was I doing the right thing? I was filled with mixed emotions, excited and fearful at the same time.

Flying over the iconic Sydney Harbour Bridge into Kingsford Smith Airport, I knew I was home. My overseas experience had come to an end. And what an experience it had been! An hour through customs and bag collection, and there was Don, waiting for me at the arrival gates. I felt a rush of relief seeing his face, although his face did look a little bit different.

Don't get me wrong: I was incredibly happy to be reunited with him. But for the first time in our relationship, Don looked old. He suddenly looked his fifty years, and the twenty-year age gap was glaringly obvious. How could I have not noticed this before? A hint of doubt entered my mind.

It was now the end of 2002, and I was almost thirty.

The next few months proved to be some of the hardest of my life—as Don had not held up his end of the bargain. Not only did he not find us a home to move into, but he had also moved back in with his estranged wife and teenage children. Arguing he hadn't been able to pull himself away from his kids, he begged me for more time. Realising how much his children missed him had caused him to feel guilty for his absence over the past year.

With no other options, I slept at my mother's house for a few weeks until my beachside apartment in Sydney's Northern Beaches became vacant. My homecoming was a complete disaster.

Don tried desperately to keep me close enough that I wouldn't walk away. He returned to his office in Sydney's Circular Quay and resumed his everyday life—except for this time, he was trying to fit me into his schedule. We attempted to have regular date nights and managed a couple of weekend getaways.

He claimed to have moved downstairs in his marital home, but I had my doubts. It didn't matter what part of the house he was sleeping in, he was living in a house with a woman he was legally bound to. I had officially become the mistress. And it didn't sit well. This was not what I had signed up for.

After several fights, disappointments, and unmet expectations, I finally gave up waiting for Don's circumstances to change. The situation was toxic and had to end. Just before Christmas, I chose to leave him until he sorted himself out. I deserved better, and I had to protect myself. I was utterly devastated.

At the same time that Don and I were breaking apart, over in New Zealand, Patsy and Nikos were also going through a separation. Simultaneously, Patsy and I were going through hell. It made sense to be together. So I jumped on a plane and headed across the ditch to meet her in Auckland. Over the next ten days, in a borrowed car, we drove all around New Zealand's North Island. We were both emotional wrecks. We cried, we laughed, we reminisced, and we cursed our exes.

Through the tears, we toured the land of the long white cloud, racking up memories and ticking off bucket list items. Like Thelma and Louise, we supported each other on the adventure of a lifetime. Fortunately, we lived to tell the stories.

In the end, Don wasn't willing to walk away freely. He wanted me, but he couldn't break away from his conventional home life. He would ring me, text me, and find ways to see me. Painfully, I had to push away the man I loved. I had to stay strong. Succumbing to the occasional catch-up over a drink, I was torn between holding onto hope that he would build a life with me and standing my ground to fight for what I believed I was worthy of. Bottom line: I had to love myself more, and that wasn't easy.

Given Don's insistence that his marriage had failed a long time ago and his declaration that he was in love with me, I found it difficult to understand why he didn't just leave. It made no sense to me. Acknowledging I had no children and no idea how tough the break-up would be, I recalled some words of wisdom from my favourite doctor: "It's better to come from a broken family than live *in* a broken family." There had to be more factors at play. Was Don telling me the truth?

I started to question why he would choose to stay in an unhappy marriage. Why choose to remain miserable, without love and affection? A raft of reasons came to mind. Not being a middle-aged man and not being married, I could only speculate.

Was it because he was accustomed to a certain standard of living and saw divorce diminishing his way of life? Was he unwilling to give up a big house in a popular neighbourhood and an established and comfortable existence to downsize and start again?

Was it the expense? Was it about status or community standing? Or was it an unshakable identity as a married family man? Was it merely the fear of being single? I have no idea and probably never will.

Don's decision to stay in his loveless marriage for the sake of his children was honourable and deserved respect, but in doing so, he gave up his right to continue his relationship with me. My birthday was at the end of January, and I was about to turn thirty. I promised myself that if Don hadn't changed his accommodation by then, I would stop all forms of communication.

And I did just that. For a whopping three weeks.

It was about ten o'clock at night on Valentine's Day when I reluctantly took Don's call. He was intoxicated. He was at his home, supposedly in his downstairs bedroom, and very upset. We were both distraught. Not coping well with our separation, he was slurring his words while telling me how much he loved me and wanted to see me. Amazingly, I was stronger than I thought. I didn't cave in. Despite his tears, I maintained my stance. I continued to refuse to see him. I was so battle-scarred by this stage, I was becoming numb and developing resilience.

I said goodnight and hopped into bed. I was proud of myself for saying no.

Around three in the morning, I was awakened by the sound of my phone ringing. It was Don. Did I really need to have this conversation again? I answered the call—only this time, it was a woman's voice at the end of the line, saying "Hello, this is Gladys, Don's wife."

Holy crap, what was going on? My heart was pounding, and I was instantly alert. Was I really on the phone with Don's wife at three in the morning? Why would she be ringing me in the middle of the night? She began by saying she wasn't a bad person, and she just wanted some answers.

Wow. Things had just gotten very real!

I was pleasant and answered most of her questions. Some I felt were not for me to answer, and I chose to plead ignorance. I did, however, explain my intentions and my understanding of Don's situation, divulging that I had moved back from Greece expecting to move in with him. Evidently, Don's home life was a lot more complicated than I had envisaged.

I'm glad I received that early-morning call. It was the slap in the face I needed. It was clear I had to immediately and permanently remove myself from Don's life. Divorce wasn't in the cards anytime soon.

My hopes were pulverised, and my heart was crushed. After litres of ice cream, kilos of chocolate, a river of tears, and truckloads of self-pity, I had to pull myself up. I was worthy of much better. I needed to get on with my life and do it quickly. I put on a brave face and an artificial smile and pretended I was okay.

Back to the drawing board. I was single yet again at thirty. I had missed my deadline. I had to pull out and amend my life plan.

Life Plan #5

1. Find and fall in love with my soulmate by the age of 32
2. Be in a relationship for 6 months before getting engaged
3. Get married at 33
4. Have my first child at 34
5. Have my second child at 35
6. Be settled in a family home with a husband and children by 36
7. Live happily ever after.

Sadly, I learned the hard lesson that *separated* does not always result in divorce.

On a deeper level, I discovered that marriage doesn't prevent loneliness. Being trapped in loveless matrimony renders you hopeless, without options or the ability to act if presented with better prospects. With no optimism and no way forward, you are just treading water. Your hands are tied; your bed is made. Being single suddenly didn't seem all that bad.

CHAPTER 8

Entering My Thirties

Maxine's birthday falls three days after mine, and since we were fifteen years old, we have celebrated our milestones together. For our thirtieth, we planned a weekend of fun with Judy for a much-needed girls-only getaway. Through thick and thin, I could count on the two of them to be there for me during my heartbreak.

A milestone birthday called for a grandiose celebration. We started the day climbing the Sydney Harbour Bridge. This was quite an accomplishment for Maxine and I, as we both suffer from a debilitating fear of heights. Straddled over the metal frame walkway, positioned high above the harbour below, Maxine and I edged our way forward on our rear ends for what seemed like an eternity. I was petrified and wanted to cry. Poor Judy was wedged between us, pulling and pushing us along until we painstakingly reached the central stairwell. Tied together, we had no option but to complete the climb.

Standing on top of the bridge felt unbelievable. Scared to look down, I tentatively took in the spectacular city views: the Opera House, the magnificent harbour, the smiling face of Luna Park, and the boats pulling into Circular Quay. What a remarkable achievement.

Maxine being a fussy eater, we chose to dine at Pancakes on the Rocks before we strolled across the city towards Darling Harbour to watch *Mamma Mia*, the musical. On a high, we topped off the night at our favourite nightclub, which housed an eighties disco.

I wasn't a big fan of the nightclub scene, particularly back in the days when smoking was permitted inside the venue. But I loved eighties music, so whenever I could influence our choice of establishment, I would always choose the eighties.

It had been a long time since I was out dancing with the girls, and I was having a ball. The nightlife scene never seemed to change. Its prime function was to be a place to find love or lust, and it was amusing to spectate.

Not long into the night, I was targeted by a man wearing a very distasteful shirt: yellow on one side, patterned on the other, a replica from the eighties era, just a touch too far. He was rather cute, with an attractive smile, but I wasn't convinced about the shirt. We engaged in small talk in a quieter corner of the venue. I was never comfortable meeting strangers at nightclubs. Unfairly, I was convinced men were only after one thing, and I was reluctant to give any man my full attention.

After a few nudges from Judy and Maxine, I allowed myself to spend some time with Mr. Eighties. Learning his name was Luigi, I discovered he was Italian, and the shirt was a dare from a friend. He claimed to be single, available, and employed. Tick. I invited him to join us on the dance floor for the remainder of the evening.

As closing time neared, Luigi kindly escorted us outside to say our goodbyes. Immediately next to the venue, a night food stall was selling fresh sausage sandwiches. The mouth-watering smell of barbequed snags lingered in the air. Excitedly, we joined the line to feast on a sausage sanga—the perfect ending to a perfect day. Luigi, however, disdainfully said he didn't eat sausages. What?

Immediate red flag! Who doesn't eat sausages? After we exchanged phone numbers, he kissed me on the cheek and went on his way.

Nursing slight hangovers, the three of us spent the next morning at my beachside apartment eating cheeses and playing Scrabble. And then the texting started. Luigi wanted to take me on a date. As flattered as I was to receive the attention, my head wasn't convinced it was a good idea. I wasn't over Don, and I couldn't get past the sausage issue. How could I ever take him to a barbeque?

Over the next three hours, Judy and Maxine beat me into submission, advising me I was too fussy and never gave men a chance. The poor guy just wanted to go on one date. Reluctantly, I caved in.

Luigi organised a midweek lunchtime date the following week. I was comfortable with this arrangement; it seemed like a safe option. Driving an hour to his local neighbourhood, I met him outside a French restaurant. I greeted him apprehensively as he escorted me inside. Looking around the room, I realised we were the only two people here.

We exchanged small talk as we ate our meal—an ordinary meal at that. My fish dish was littered with delicate bones; not a great look picking bones out of my teeth on a first date. Keen to get out of there, we headed for the cash register, where Luigi proceeded to pay for my meal using a shop-a-docket—a two-for-one deal printed on the back of a grocery store receipt. Ouch! I was immediately embarrassed and outright horrified. I acknowledge he was being thrifty, *but seriously*, on a first date? I should have run a mile right then and there.

But I didn't. I reminded myself of Maxine and Judy's insistence that I didn't give men a chance. I pushed through a long line of red flags and spent the next three months with Luigi. He was generous, and he did mean well, but I was never going to fall in love. Time to be single again. Luigi was a short-lived distraction.

Failure to Launch

Turning thirty signified the failure of my original life plan, and I quietly started to panic. Celebrating my friends getting married over the past few years had been lovely, but I was sad I wasn't the one walking down the aisle. Why wasn't it happening for me? Envy was creeping in. I was sincerely over the moon for my girlfriends but simultaneously gutted it wasn't me.

Now, at thirty, a wave of my close friends began having children. They were new mums, and they were smitten. They had secured their happily-ever-after. It was a struggle to watch.

If I thought spending time with couples was hard as a single woman, spending time with couples and their children was much harder. I was constantly reminded of what I didn't have and how far behind I was in the race. Like playing Monopoly, I kept being sent back to *Go*. I was yet again back at the starting line.

Since I was the odd one out, the misfit, the third wheel, my friends were keen to get me on track. Conversations once again were focussed purely on my relationship status.

"How's your love life?"

"Have you met anyone?"

"Are you putting yourself out there?"

It was the same questions over and over again for what seemed like an eternity. An edge of pity kept creeping into the dialogue.

"Poor thing."

"I'm sorry you're on your own."

I had been here before. It was déjà vu.

I became the nuisance child who was always in the way. Frustrated by my single predicament, my friends reminded me that I was too fussy, suggesting it was all my fault. They kept sending subtle hints that I should lower my standards to "fix" my problem.

Never mind it takes two people to form a relationship; it was clearly on me to get my act together and sort things out. I appreciated that their comments came from a place of love and a desire for me to be happy, but they left me feeling like I was to blame.

On a subconscious level, their messages reinforced what society had embedded in me as a child: *You can't be happy and fulfilled on your own. You are not complete until you find a man.*

Sometimes I felt the barrage of questions was their way of making sure I wasn't burying my head in the sand and that I was actively trying to resolve my issue—my single status; that I was taking the task seriously; and that I was, indeed, searching for a companion and not just lazing around.

The truth was, I found it difficult to admit that I fancied someone. It was hard enough suffering unrequited love, processing my rejections in private, dealing with my issues of self-worth and *why not me.* I certainly didn't want to live that rejection on a stage in front of all my friends and family. I didn't want to share my hopes and love interests with all and sundry, only to have them watch the real-time rejection—voyeurism of a new kind, watching a poor soul offering herself to a man, only to be knocked down in flames.

No. I wasn't having a bar of that. If I liked a boy, I was keeping that information to only a very privileged few. My failed love life was not for others' entertainment.

Fortunately, I did have a kindred spirit in Maxine, who found herself single after a broken engagement. Although she lived four hours away, I took solace in knowing I wasn't the only woman who had failed to launch.

Without a local wing-woman, I had to carve out my own path. The problem was that I just wasn't meeting any prospects. Options were limited, and I had no idea where to search. Now and then,

I travelled down to visit Maxine, who regularly frequented the Canberra nightclub strip.

Nightclubs were a double-edged sword. I loved dancing, and I loved catching up with my girlfriends, but I didn't like sacrificing my weekend daylight hours to catch up on sleep and rid my body of alcohol. Not that I ever drank too much. Three times in my life, I can put my hand on my heart and admit I was over the limit, trashed, or quite simply, drunk. Perhaps that's what I was doing wrong: I attended the nightclubs sober!

Being sober afforded me much entertainment. Observing people interact and mingle was like watching a scene from the Discovery Channel, with men indiscreetly attempting to pick up every living, breathing woman in the room without success (not exactly hand-picking someone special). Intoxicated women threw themselves at men who didn't even bother asking their names. Then there were the husband-hunting antics and the closing-time scramble of drunken bodies trying to find someone to take home. I watched it all.

It was a jungle out there, and it was brutal. On the rare occasion when I started a conversation with a possible suitor, I found myself having to roll off a ten-minute questionnaire just to figure out if said man was actually available. I couldn't just ask if he was single; as history had taught me, each man has his own unique definition of that status. I had to ask a range of questions:

- "Are you married?"
- "Are you engaged?"
- "Are you living with a woman?"
- "Do you have a girlfriend?"
- "Are you seeing anyone?"
- "Are you emotionally available?"

A missed question could result in a strategic omission of fact and a subsequent waste of my time. Many men were hedging their bets or playing the market. I needed to be savvy.

And wedding rings: what is it with married men not wearing wedding rings? As a single woman, my first glance is always at a man's ring finger. No ring means fair game. It is hard enough finding a decent man without wasting an hour chatting with a potential only to find he neglected to wear the one thing that declared his commitment. Not a level playing field!

Albeit amusing to watch, others' alcohol-fuelled attempts to find love left me feeling incredibly miserable and disheartened. Nightclubs were not the place I was going to find *the one*. So where was I supposed to find him?

In my perception of reality, there were simply no men left. More specifically, there were no single, eligible, emotionally available men who were attracted to me. All the good ones were taken. I was completely convinced of this. The evidence didn't lie. I had spent significant energy and time searching for the right partner, to no avail. My results were proof. I was single, childless, and in my thirties.

Left on a platter was an array of duds for me to sift through. Slim pickings. Perhaps these dud men felt the same way about me? I was beginning to believe my true soulmate had given up trying to find me and settled for his backup plan. Alas, I was destined to live the rest of my life alone.

Left on the Shelf

Work was my primary success in life. I always managed to land on my feet. Returning from Greece, I started a new venture. Don may have broken my heart, but upon my return to Australia, he was instrumental in helping me create my own business. He believed in my abilities, supported, and encouraged me. He changed the course of my career, and for this, I am eternally grateful.

Through my new business, I landed a contract working in Sydney city, on the doorstep of Darling Harbour. During my lunch hour, I would circle the harbour, people-watching as the boats came into the dock. The office itself was small, with free wine and beer supplied every Friday evening. A tremendous little vibe was forming.

I sat next to Glen. He was a dedicated worker in his mid-forties and had been faithfully married to Karen for more than twenty years. Having met Karen on a couple of occasions, I found her to be warm, caring, and beautiful. They had two teenage sons, a house in the suburbs, and a pet dog. They were living their happily-ever-after. They were settled. Glen's face would light up when he spoke proudly of his wife and his children; he was filled with joy. He had the entire package—the package that had somehow continued to elude me.

One day at work, in the spirit of getting to know me better, Glen enquired about my home life and my significant other. He was genuinely interested in learning more about me and my circumstances. In hindsight, I believe he had a preconceived idea that I was happily partnered with prospects of forthcoming children on the horizon. This idea, however, was far from my reality.

I proceeded to describe in detail my current life situation, being single at thirty-one with no potential suitors in the midst. Glen's response left me in shock. Visually, he appeared to be very upset upon learning of my situation. His face fell sullen, and his voice quivered as he replied, "You've been left on the shelf." He was clearly distressed and couldn't bring himself to shield his disappointment with what he saw as my failure.

I wasn't quite sure how to respond. I was torn between a sudden urge to calm his distress and a desire to justify my lack of performance and convince him he was wrong.

When the words came out of his mouth, I pictured myself as a cabbage that had gone to seed. It was too late for me. I had been left too long without being picked. My chances of finding my happily-ever-after, according to Glen, were over. Any feelings about me being a failure were now cemented in stone.

CHAPTER 9

Biological Clock Kicks In

Spending more and more time with my friends' children caused a shift in me. Babies had never triggered me to gush and goo and go baby crazy. I never disliked babies; I just didn't drop everything to hold one. Judy would often joke about not using me as a babysitter due to my delayed desire for motherhood. Yes, I wanted my own family, but I was focussed on finding *the one* before thinking too much about children.

Until, that is, I met Lucas. Lucas was two, an inquisitive blonde-haired boy belonging to my friend Sally. Sally was going through marital issues and one day landed on my doorstep with Lucas. They spent the next four months living with me in my beachside apartment.

For the first time, I delighted in spending time with a little person. Most mornings, I would make him scrambled eggs for breakfast, and then we would sit together to watch cartoons.

I developed quite a fondness for Lucas during that period. My motherly instincts finally kicked in. I remember his night-time routine: Sally would tuck him into bed and gently close the door. Within a few minutes, he would quietly get up and open the door, standing in the doorway without a word. It was his protest at being sent to bed. He held his ground, motionless, waiting for one of us to notice him and send him back. He never did venture past that point. He was brave enough to stand up for his convictions but smart enough not to push the boundary any further. He was so adorable, I couldn't help but fall in love.

That was the moment I genuinely wanted to become a mum. I wanted my own family. I had gained an appreciation of what I would miss out on if I didn't find a man. I started to imagine what it would be like to grow and nurture my own child, my own kin.

It was the trigger for my biological clock to start ticking. Abruptly, it dawned on me that I could be running out of time.

My life plan had now hit a critical point. At thirty-two, the sound of my clock was irrefutable. It was like a time bomb had been activated inside my womb. Suddenly, I realised my eggs had a definitive expiry date. Why had I not noticed this before? Time was now of the essence. I began to feel spasms of panic.

My biological clock proceeded to play havoc with my thoughts and emotions, like a plague affecting my entire body. My reasoning during this period was questionable and perhaps contributed to a string of unrequited loves. Before the pounding of my clock, I had stayed faithful to my list of must-haves in a partner and a relationship. Regardless of my life-plan deadline, I wasn't willing to compromise my values. Each time I walked away from a relationship, I simply pushed out my life plan. The rest of my life, I had assumed, would be a very long time, and I had convinced myself I was worthy of finding the right man, not just any man.

That was, of course, until the sounds of my clock muffled the rational voices inside my head and I began to lower my standards. Fear was starting to take over, and time was now more critical than criteria on a checklist. I dropped my bar to allow myself to consider more potentials—men I would never have given a second glance to in my twenties. A hint of desperation had set in. The landscape was now changed. My ticking clock became an evil demon spreading to the extremities of my being. My confidence plummeted, self-doubt set in, and fear took over. The urgency was at the forefront of my mind. Forget my long-held ideals; I was now in a race to beat my biological clock.

Holiday Escape

Maxine needed a wing-woman, and I welcomed a break from my ticking bomb. It was time to take my annual holiday. Maxine was planning her own overseas trip, so we decided to coordinate our itineraries to meet up in Cardiff, Wales.

Departing earlier, I spent three weeks touring Central America with a group of travellers on an adventure tour. Setting out from Guatemala City, we traversed Honduras, Belize, and through to Cancun, Mexico, enjoying daily pina coladas while unearthing the history of the Mayan civilization.

As promised, I landed in Cardiff; which just happened to be the city where Maxine's recent love interest resided. I was her dutiful chaperone.

We met up with Maxine's beau at a popular nightclub. My two-glass-a-night alcohol limit, however, did not prepare me for the onslaught of shots being thrown my way. Maxine's Welsh potential seemed charming and sported very generous friends. On our inaugural night in Cardiff, I gifted them with my second lifetime experience of being completely wasted—so wasted, I couldn't exit the ladies' room.

I sadly let Australia down, proving I couldn't handle my alcohol. I had to be escorted from the complex by a man I had met only hours earlier—thankfully, a respectable man who delivered me to my hotel room. Maxine had left me for dead. She was still inside wooing her Welsh boy.

Following a week of complete submersion into the Welsh drinking culture, my body needed a rest. Leaving Maxine to find her feet, I continued on to Surrey to catch up with Zoe before heading up to Norwich to visit Patsy. I loved returning to England, with its thatched-roof cottages, proudly restored castles, and narrow country roads with buildings abutting the pavement. Everything was so old. Knowing I was amidst centuries of history, centuries of war, and royal sagas was so fascinating. Most of all, I loved catching up with my girlfriends.

I ended my trip with a stopover in Thailand. Maxine flew in to accompany me on, you guessed it, an adventure tour. Thai food is my favourite cuisine, and nothing compares to the real deal. Feasting on pad thai and red curry, my taste buds were in heaven. We spent four days trekking through the jungle north of Chiang Mai. Maxine still curses me to this day for finding amusement in her sinking knee-deep into the mud as we hiked up one of the mountains. Greeted by village women eager to offer a massage in exchange for a meagre payment, we played cards by candlelight and slept under mosquito nets in barns where I could see and hear chickens and other livestock running around under the widely spaced timber floorboards—unforgettable memories.

Sadly, Maxine's Welsh potential was not a long-term prospect, so together we conjured up a plan for future travel. This time, we decided to buy four tickets to the 2007 Rugby World Cup in France, giving us two spare tickets. The intention was for each of us to find a significant other to take on the trip. We had approximately eighteen months to seal the deal. Surely a single woman bearing Rugby World Cup tickets could secure a boyfriend?

I promptly updated my life plan.

Life Plan #6

1. Find and fall in love with my soulmate by the age of 33
2. Be in a relationship for 6 months before getting engaged
3. Get married at 34
4. Have my first child at 35
5. Have my second child at 36
6. Live happily ever after.

CHAPTER 10

A Welcome Relief

Thirty-two, single, and childless, I welcomed the opportunity to move to Melbourne on a new work contract. It was a chance to break the dating drought and something to look forward to—a new chapter.

Melbourne, voted several times the world's most liveable city, lived up to its reputation. Sprawling with trams, the city was enveloped in a hive of activity. I enjoyed award-winning restaurants, a continuous program of cultural and sporting events, and a sea of friendly faces. There was a wonderful heart to Melbourne.

Working in the event industry alongside many single career-minded individuals, I had found my tribe. I breathed a sigh of relief. Immersing myself into my new role, I took the opportunity to join in the vast array of organised social gatherings. There was never a shortage of festivities to tag along to. Life was getting better.

Optimistically, I began to scour the ocean of single Melbourne men. Maxine had set me up with her long-time friend Anne, who showed me the ropes, provided weekend entertainment, and introduced me to a raft of potentials. Although she was in a relationship herself, she was the ideal wing-woman.

Sean worked with Anne. He was playful, good-looking, and single. Tick. We engaged in friendly and flirtatious banter over a sequence of Friday-night drinks. And then we extended the banter over a couple of date nights. But nothing further progressed. Sean was too busy spreading his flirtatious offerings to other single women. No worries; only one month wasted. Plenty more fish in this Melbourne sea.

My attention was then drawn to Patrick, another introduction from Anne. Patrick was ruggedly handsome and a little shy around me. He was a good friend of Anne's partner, and so I would find reasons to pop over for visits. We barely spent any time alone or had any opportunity to delve into a serious conversation, but Patrick's physical presence gave me goosebumps. He was the perfect size—stocky and a head-height taller than me. I felt protected in his presence, a feeling I relished.

One afternoon, we were finally left alone in the lounge room. Great! We could finally talk. But no, we didn't speak. Instead, Patrick stood up, walked over, and kissed me. Wow! I hadn't seen that coming. And what a marvellous kiss! Soft, sensual, lingering ... perfect. He grabbed my hand and didn't let go all evening.

Smitten, I was back in the game. Woohoo! Thirty-two and about to start another relationship. Or was I? After less than twenty-four hours of euphoria, Patrick broke the news. "I really like you, but ..."

Oh dear, here we go again, I thought.

"But our timing is crap," he said. "I have just started a long-distance relationship with another girl, and I really need to give her a chance. I wish we had gotten together weeks ago. I'm sorry."

Okay, I now believed there was something really wrong with me. This was not a coincidence. Either the universe was punishing me, or my judgement skills were abysmal. Either way, I needed to sort myself out.

Having been down this road before, I knew what to do. I put on a brave face, smiled, and wished Patrick well, hiding my disappointment and damaged pride. I was grateful we had only kissed—a memorable kiss at that. Still, it was two more months wasted.

Anne's collection of potentials was seemingly impaired, so I chose to search further afield. Work was a prominent battleground. In front of me was an assortment of single men from all over the globe. I decided to explore the pasture.

Pete was lovely. He took charge and commanded authority and was also my official office hugger. Whenever I needed a hug, I went to Pete. Any time of the day, I could count on him for affection. Some of my work colleagues could see our potential and were keen to set us up. I was a willing participant, but Pete not so. Okay, next…

Mark was incredibly handsome and didn't know it. He was laid-back, with a love of travel. In fact, he was one of the very few prospects who loved travelling more than I did; it was his number-one passion. Hmm … I definitely needed to get to know him better.

But wait—I wasn't the only woman vying for his attention. His humble approach was no disguise, and other women saw what I saw. When I found out several junior staff members were chasing Mark, I had to slide away quickly. That could have been very embarrassing. Competing with my subordinates for the attention of a man was not congruous to the professional image I wanted to portray. Mark was definitely not a viable option.

Okay, next … and next again. Wherever I turned, I was overlooked or beaten to the prize by younger women. Melbourne turned out to be a revolving door of unrequited affection. Constantly friend-zoned, I was racking up a resume of single mates.

I took comfort in my friendship with Will, who was eight years my junior. An Englishman, he had moved to Australia for work with his girlfriend in tow. I spent many Friday nights hanging out with him after the usual crowd dispersed. We went dancing, played games in the amusement arcade, and talked for hours. Will was honourable and never stepped across the mateship boundary. In another time and place, things might have been different, or maybe not. I enjoyed our friendship, and I could temporarily forget I was single.

After fifteen months of social participation, I felt defeated and emotionally depleted. I was tired of investing energy in meeting new men, flirting and getting to know them, only to keep ending up back at square one. This cycle was exhausting. My optimism waned. It appeared I really had been left on the shelf.

Now thirty-three, I was old in comparison to my youthful competition. Perhaps I was trying too hard or was too available— just not elusive enough to be desirable? Whatever the reason, it just wasn't happening for me.

I was grateful for the perpetual calendar of social work gatherings, but I would rather have been at home on the couch snuggled up to a significant other. But to do that, I had to put myself out there to meet my significant other, be in the game, be seen, meet people, and find *the one*. It was a catch-22.

I needed to change my strategy. All was not lost. I was still holding on to my Rugby World Cup tickets.

CHAPTER 11

Single Married Mother or Not?

After eighteen months in Melbourne, I found myself no closer to a relationship. I had one week left on my work assignment. I was thirty-three and still single.

It was the closing ceremony night of the 2006 Commonwealth Games, and the city was buzzing with excitement. Melbourne was celebrating its successful hosting of the games, and I was soaking up the atmosphere.

My dear friend Suzy joined me at the stadium to watch the ceremony. Suzy and I were similar in age, both single, and worked together. She would often sleep over at my place on weekends due to my proximity to the tram network.

After the ceremony, we headed into the city on foot along with thousands of other revellers. Joining us was Alan, our affable new friend who had introduced himself when sitting next to us at the stadium. Alan was a visitor to Melbourne looking to continue his evening frivolity. We figured it was harmless to invite him to join us.

I felt immediately at ease in Alan's presence. We landed at our designated after-party with other work colleagues, and I stole Alan's attention for most of the night. I established quickly that he was an intelligent man, he was recently single, and he lived in Tasmania. He seemed quite nice. Poor Suzy was subsequently relegated to wing-woman for the evening.

Alan and I indulged in a passionate embrace before exchanging numbers. We then continued to meet up for the next three days before Alan's departure. Being one to never say no to a challenging situation, I found a way to continue our story. Fast-forward three months, I had a new job in a small town in South East Queensland, and Alan and I were in a long-distance relationship.

And yes, he was willing to accompany me to the Rugby World Cup. I was thirty-three.

Long-Distance Challenges

Alan was gregarious and uber-confident, with a powerful intellect. He commanded attention in any room. Our relationship was solid, but we were faced with many hurdles.

Initially, our long-distance relationship spanned three states of Australia. In the beginning, we managed flights back and forth on weekends. But after a couple of months, I quit my full-time job in exchange for a flexible contract that saw me work only three-and-a-half days per week. This allowed me to fly to Tasmania for three-day weekends so we could spend quality time together. At first, I didn't mind. I was happy to do all the flying—whatever was needed to grow the relationship.

Things were progressing well. Six months along, however, we were faced with a make-or-break dilemma. Alan landed an opportunity to work overseas in South East Asia. I had some immediate decisions

85

to make. Could our relationship last with an even more significant distance between us? Was I willing to put in even more effort?

Having worked overseas, I knew the job would offer an incredibly rewarding life experience for Alan. Struggling already with the energy required to maintain our long-distance romance, I was disappointed that our living arrangements were about to get worse. But I knew if the shoe was on the other foot, I would want Alan to support my growth, so I had to encourage him to go. I wasn't ready to lose him; I just had to remain optimistic we would get through this and find ways to make the relationship work. We would just have to adapt.

As the months progressed, my optimism waned. A four-week-on, two-week-off, fly-in fly-out roster didn't offer us much time together. I found myself in a long line of people wanting to commandeer Alan in the limited time he had back in Australia. His two-week breaks were jam-packed with social gatherings in his home town with his friends and family. Disappointingly, my friends and my family were not on the priority list and rarely got to spend much time with us as a couple.

One of my favourite pastimes is camping. For many years, a group of us, including Maxine and Judy, had come together for camping trips over the Christmas and Easter holidays. These trips were an excuse to let our hair down, play cards and board games, drink, laugh, and be silly. Many extraordinary memories have come from our camping ventures. And sadly, Alan never featured in those memories.

Our long-distance romance left me on my own during the holidays. Alan was always missing in action. This made me sad and often lonely. I was in a relationship, yet I felt very alone. It wasn't just the camping; it was all the significant milestones he was missing— the birthdays, friends' weddings, Christmas lunches. Yet again, I felt like I was living my life as a single woman. I was making a lot of sacrifices.

What we did share was a love of travel. After three months in Laos, Alan changed his roster to on-site residency, which included a double-storey white brick house in Vientiane, within security fences, and a guard called Oum. Oum was a gentle and quiet man who resided in a sparsely furnished room connected to the back of the house. It had a concrete floor, running water, and barely enough room for a canvas stretcher bed. This was sadly how the hired help lived.

The changed roster gave me a reason to travel to Laos for five-week intervals: five weeks in Laos, five weeks in Oz. Alan's new roster, now ten days on, four days off, seemed too good to be true. And it was. No sooner had I arrived for my first vacation than Alan was deployed permanently to the mine site, some four hours into the jungle. Great! Now I was alone in a massive house, in a foreign country where I didn't speak the local language, for ten days at a time. Twenty-three days out of my thirty-five-day visit, I was completely solo, except for Oum. The universe was not being kind. Thankfully, I had internet access.

Oum was now the guard, the maid, and the gardener. Expats were expected to offer wages to the local community, and it made sense to extend these offerings to my reliable helper. Incredibly placid, Oum taught me the basics of Buddhism.

On Alan's four-day breaks, he and I would steal away to neighbouring countries. At least I was expanding my travel portfolio.

A Change of Scenery

Chasing the expatriate life; when the Laos job ended, Alan found a replacement position in Johannesburg, South Africa, on a full-time assignment. This change happened to coincide with the end of my flexible work contract. I had to find new employment. Unable to secure a similar arrangement, I chose a position in Rockhampton, Central Queensland, where I succeeded in negotiating a nine-week holiday into my contract.

Rockhampton, the self-proclaimed beef capital of Australia, is full of warm and welcoming locals. With Alan in South Africa full-time, I was once again experiencing life in solitude. I found my feet and was living on my own at thirty-four.

Alan and I had an informal agreement. I consented to two years of long-distance love in return for future family life, including marriage and children. Given my age, it was only fair that my needs were considered too, albeit delayed temporarily. I only had to wait two years. My ultimatum to Alan was that he had two years to figure out if he wanted to marry me. If that wasn't enough time, then clearly, I wasn't the one for him.

After almost two years to the day, as we sat precariously on a chairlift spanning the picturesque Launceston Gorge, Alan presented me with a ring and said, "Will you marry me?" As I was afraid of heights, and concentrating for dear life on staying put in the rocking chair, it took me a few seconds to digest the question. "Yes, yes, I will," I cautiously replied.

And just like that, we were engaged. There was no kiss, no passion, just a formal verbal contract to enter into a marriage. Perhaps Alan was nervous? We hopped off the chairlift—I was relieved to be back on solid ground—and strolled around to the other side of the gorge. By this stage, I was feeling disheartened. "You haven't even kissed me yet," I declared.

"Oh, sorry," he replied and then quickly puckered up, pressing his lips against mine for a mere two seconds.

It was an incredibly romantic setting, and later I discovered the proposal was a rehearsed plan. But I was disappointed. There was no longing look into each other's eyes, no all-encompassing hug squeezing the life out of each other—in fact, there was no hug at all. After years of anticipation, I was sadly a little empty, but I couldn't let Alan know. I knew his intentions were honourable. He had done his best, and I felt terrible for feeling dissatisfied. Then back to South Africa he flew.

My Turn to Choose

Our relationship was built on love and respect, but like all couples, we had our own unique issues. Some of those issues lingered for years unresolved. Spending extended periods apart, we barely had time to air our grievances. Our time together was precious, so our problems had to wait.

Nine weeks in South Africa, the land of electric fences and driving through red lights, was intriguing—and scary at times. I was grateful for my life in Australia. With the stark contrast between poverty-stricken shanty towns and affluent gated communities, Johannesburg had a diverse and heart-wrenching history.

Escaping to Maputo, Mozambique, for a short break, we chose to splurge on five-star lodgings. Joining the hotel's organised city tour, we met an English gentleman in his eighties who aspired to travel to every country—every single one! A banker in his earlier days, his work had taken him abroad. Now he was closing in on his goal; Mozambique was country 174. He was in his eighties and determined to fulfil his life dream. I was so incredibly inspired and in awe of this man. What an outstanding achievement!

Vastly impressed, I was instantly motivated to adopt a similar life goal. I decided that I, too, wanted a target. I made the decision then and there that I wanted to get to 100 countries in my lifetime.

Abruptly and without warning, Alan's job in South Africa came to a premature end. Reluctantly, he came home to Australia to live with me in Rockhampton. Finally, it was my turn. I had earnt my stripes. I had patiently waited in the background. Now I could finally call the shots. I wanted a baby. I wanted stability, at least for a few years. After fifteen years in the workforce with an accomplished career, I felt I was deserving of some time off.

As I was now financially supporting both of us, I was keen for Alan to find employment. In Rockhampton, prospects were limited. We were, however, building a house on the outskirts of Brisbane, so it made sense to focus our energies there.

Struggling with his immersion back into normal life, Alan delayed looking for work. One evening, on our daily walk, he confessed, "Babe, I can't go back to working a nine-to-five-job." *What?* I immediately stopped breathing. "What do you mean?" I asked, although his statement was obvious. "I can't go back to normal working life. I can't do the five-day-a-week job ever again. It won't make me happy; I just can't do it." It turned out Alan was addicted to the excitement of expatriate life. He wanted the thrill of a remote and exotic location.

My heart sank, and I felt a massive pain in my stomach. I couldn't believe what I was hearing. I was devastated. What happened to it being my turn? What happened to his commitment to family life, together, in the same location, at the same address? Had I just invested two and a half years of my life for nothing? I just wanted to go home and cry.

Hoping Alan would have a change of heart, I proceeded to find a new work assignment in Brisbane, and together we moved into our newly built home. Resentment, however, was starting to manifest. Alan was now a kept spouse (or spouse-to-be) with no ambition to take on a permanent local role. How did my life get to this?

Alan wanted the adrenalin rush attached to the big overseas assignments. He enjoyed his fly-in, fly-out life. He craved the mateship embedded in male-dominated mine sites. He had become spoilt. Like a child with his favourite toy, he was not giving up. As clear as day, I now knew our lifestyle choices would never align. I was thirty-five with two clear options in front of me:

1. Marry Alan and become a single married mother—a married woman whose husband is never home, bringing up her children alone, without physical support. Thrown in for good measure would be occasional visits from a husband who was living an exotic life without me. I visualised an incredibly lonely and difficult path. A married life on paper, a single life in reality. Or ...

2. Believe that I was worthy of realising my dreams of companionship and family union, which could only be achieved by walking away, breaking up with Alan, and finding a man who wanted to share my life vision. I would become a single woman at thirty-five, knowing I had limited time to have children but having the potential to find someone who would be physically present to share my life with.

The decision weighed on me. I acknowledged that I couldn't change Alan, and I didn't want to. His determination and capacity to get what he wanted were qualities I loved about him. I couldn't expect him now to submit to a lifestyle he had no desire for. I was sad about my options.

Suddenly, all the faults in our relationship became magnified. Our swept-under-the-carpet issues began to suffocate me. I could hardly breathe. Our unresolved issues were now front and centre.

The problems we had avoided for the past two years were glaring at us, and we were forced to finally confront them.

We embarked on relationship counselling. But personally, I was starting to look at what else was out there. I was preparing myself for the inevitable.

Did I want to fight to keep our relationship together when that meant I was fighting to have a husband I would never see? Was I delaying an inevitable break-up? I didn't enjoy all my years feeling like the third wheel; did I really want to commit the rest of my life to attending celebrations on my own? Did I want to go through a messy divorce with children?

In the back of my mind, I kept playing over the options. Did I want to become a single married mother? I wouldn't be getting a husband to physically share my life with; I would be getting legally bound to a man I loved but would hardly ever see. Should I leave, or should I stay?

I awoke one day with a feeling of panic. The wedding plans were in motion. The date and the venue were locked in. Some friends had already booked their flights. With the apprehension inside me, I couldn't buy a wedding dress. It just didn't feel right.

And then it hit me like a punch in the stomach. The wind was forced from my body, and I could hardly breathe. I couldn't go ahead with this. I had to leave, and I was petrified. I didn't want to break Alan's heart, but my heart had already broken away.

On Remembrance Day in 2008, while strolling through the city, we stopped to rest, perching ourselves on top of a concrete retaining wall. Spontaneously, a wave of courage swept over me. I began to speak my truth. Cold and emotionless, I ended the relationship. I told Alan I couldn't go through with the wedding because I wasn't in love with him anymore and I wanted out. It was not my best work.

I just wanted to rip the Band-Aid off quickly and swiftly move on to my next chapter.

I didn't want to deal with the tidal wave of pain I had left behind. I was genuinely sorry to break Alan's heart, but I didn't want to hang around to view the aftermath, so I promptly moved out. Zoe had returned home from England and lived close to Brisbane city centre. Her spare room became my temporary new home.

Did I make the right decision? No time to doubt. I was two months off from thirty-six. Dusting off the life plan, I hastily rearranged the milestones.

Life Plan #7

1. Find and fall in love with my soulmate at the age of 36
2. Get engaged within 6 months
3. Get pregnant at 37
4. Have my first child at 38
5. Have my second child at 39
6. Get married at 40
7. Live happily ever after.

CHAPTER 12

Catalysts Are Not the Answer

In the weeks preceding the demise of my engagement, the universe presented a catalyst by the name of Jeff. *Catalyst* is the label I give to a man whose affection I crave while in the darkest moments of a troubled relationship—a forbidden desire.

It hasn't happened often, but in the past, when I found myself even remotely attracted to another man while in a relationship, I took heed, swiftly evaluating my current partnership to identify what was missing and how to address the deficiencies. Catalysts are a wake-up call, a turning point, forcing me to confront any shortcomings head-on. They're a sign prompting me to air my grievances before it's too late.

Some problems, however, were unfixable, and some relationships were never going to work regardless of how much effort I put into negotiation and compromise. Under these circumstances, I have allowed myself to indulge in a fantasy. Like a rebound, a catalyst is a mechanism to emotionally distance myself from my current partner, making it easier to walk away.

94

Don't Date the Catalyst

Jeff was my beacon of hope. We had developed a friendship through business dealings. I had found comfort in our extended conversations. Respectful not to touch on my relationship woes, we talked broadly about life in general and his love of sports. I had asked enough questions to know he was single—completely single.

Jeff was reserved, soft-spoken, and underestimated—all the things Alan wasn't. He represented a full pendulum swing. After boldly (or cruelly) ending my engagement, I was temporarily injected with a bout of fearlessness. I felt invincible.

It was just a few weeks after my break-up with Alan when I told Jeff I was now single, hoping to gauge his reaction. With my newfound confidence, I decided to be brave. What the heck—I had nothing to lose except my pride. It was getting late when Jeff and I were walking back from a business meeting one evening. As we were about to cross the road, I plucked up the courage and asked, "Do you want to have dinner with me?"

"Sure" was the response, and we immediately turned into a side street to find a local restaurant. I chose a known Italian place I had frequented with Zoe, and we sat down to enjoy our handmade pasta. Amidst the conversation, I blurted out, "I really like you, Jeff."

Phew, that felt good to get out. But Jeff didn't seem to react. *Hmm ...* I then further explained, "What I'm trying to say is: I like you a lot, more than just a friend."

Wow, that was valiant. Internally impressed with my gutsy admission, I confidently awaited a response. But Jeff just looked at me, perplexed.

In my head, when I had run this scenario over and over, I had imagined a gleeful response, a moment of excitement, at least a *yay*. Instead, I was facing someone in shock. Like a deer in headlights,

Jeff sat motionless. My recent flirting attempts had clearly gone unnoticed, like water off a duck's back. And now, sitting before me, he looked somewhat uncomfortable.

After digesting the information presented to him for what seemed like an eternity, Jeff decided we should see more of each other and see where it led. I wasn't exactly flattered by that response. But what could I do? At least he didn't run.

I now had a deeper appreciation for the men in my life who had previously plucked up the courage to ask me out. This was hard work!

Committed to making a go of it, Jeff and I spent the next three months as a couple. We enjoyed each other's company, but I was slowly discovering he was holding on to some serious baggage. In my rush to the finish line, I had forgotten to ask him some vital questions—I neglected to ask if he wanted to get married (again), I neglected to ask if he wanted children and I neglected to ask about his vision of where and how he wanted to live. Fatal mistake!

Regardless of the fun times we shared, the laughs and the engaging conversations, I could only see a dead end. Jeff definitely didn't want to remarry ever again, and he was insistent that he didn't want kids. Bugger!

Three months of my limited time vanished, although we did walk away with a friendship. And my consolation was a wonderful trip to Japan together—another country ticked off my list. Then it was back to square one for me.

A lesson to self: don't date the catalyst! Their purpose is to give me hope for what might lie ahead, not to be *the one*.

CHAPTER 13

Single Woman, Childless, and Over Thirty-Five: SWC35+

I was now a single, childless woman, age thirty-six. Unbeknownst to me, I had just contracted a disease.

Living on my own in a two-storey terraced abode north of Brisbane, I caught the train into the city each day. After work, I accompanied Zoe on an hour-long power-walk along the banks of the Brisbane River. I loved our evening catch-ups.

Zoe was dating George, an accountant who lived further south and came to visit her once a fortnight, which meant I had her to myself every second weekend. All my other girlfriends were interstate with their husbands or husbands-to-be.

As we were too old for clubbing, our weekends comprised of trips to the local markets, fine dining, and movies at the local vintage cinema. It was a pleasant and simple life, although one without access to potential single men.

SWC35+: the New Disease

The year was 2009, and Tinder was not yet a thing. My eggs were about to expire, and I was disheartened that I wasn't meeting any prospects. My friends, frustrated that I had walked away from my engagement, had given up hope. It was clearly too late for me; the tone of their voices said it all.

I no longer heard encouragement or excitement over a new crush. The curiosity about my love life had subsided. There were no more questions about finding *the one*. The answers were just too sad. The race was over, and I never crossed the finish line. I had been scratched. Emanating consolation and empathy, my friends and family simply accepted my plight. They now categorised me as a spinster.

Acquaintances would occasionally ask in passing about my family—my supposed partner and children. Given my age, it was a logical presumption. "Oh, no," I would declare. "I'm single, and I don't have children yet." I chose to include the word *yet* as a statement of intent. Responses ranged from a flimsy smile and nod to the unconvincing throwaway line, "Oh, don't worry, love, you will meet someone. You still have time." Their body language suggested otherwise: *Poor woman ...*

The pity was difficult to swallow. I was already secretly petrified without having to witness the despair and hopelessness displayed on the person in front of me. I had enough sorrow of my own without the addition of someone else's sympathy compounding my suffering.

Describing myself as a childless single woman over the age of thirty-five was like admitting I had the plague. I was cursed. Somehow, I had caught this disease: Single Woman, Childless, and Over Thirty-Five syndrome, or SWC35+, as I affectionately termed it.

My condition was wreaking havoc on my love life. On the occasions I could summon a wing-woman to accompany me on a night out, I couldn't get away from the stigma of my disease. If I thought finding a man in my early thirties was hard, suffering from SWC35+ made it a hundred times harder.

I was once told that men can sense fear in a woman like a lion and its prey. On my feeble attempts to chat-up a suitor, I couldn't escape my disposition. I was thirty-six and wanted to be in a relationship yesterday, and no matter how hard I tried to conceal it, the scent of my desperation lingered in the air.

Good men don't date women in their mid-thirties who want children. And why would they? Let's be real here. Why would any man put himself under significant time pressure to be with a woman he hardly knows, a woman who is sitting precariously on top of a biological time bomb, who wants children but has months, weeks, days, or even minutes before her eggs expire? Surely a man with plenty of offerings would opt for an easier road, a safer option, a woman who has more years of reproductive reliability. It is an obvious choice. A man would choose a woman who could give him space and time to freely grow and nurture a relationship, not put himself in a situation where he would be under instant pressure to meet his new partner's biological clock.

I canvassed my male friends and colleagues in their late thirties and asked if they were presented with two lovely single childless ladies to take on a date, one in her late twenties and one in her mid-thirties; which one would they choose? They all agreed they would opt for the woman who posed the least amount of stress and pressure. They would choose the younger woman—advocating that starting a new relationship already had obstacles and challenges without adding time-pressure fuel to the fire.

So that was that. My SWC35+ had a terminal prognosis. I was doomed.

As something to look forward to, I purchased two tickets to the 2010 FIFA World Cup being held in South Africa.

CHAPTER 14

The Insurance Plan

Time was my enemy. I was clutching just the tiniest thread of hope. Decades of happily-ever-after fantasies weren't going away in a hurry. I needed a strategy to buy myself some time. I needed to silence my ticking time bomb.

My evil clock was corrupting my thoughts and decisions as my self-esteem waned. How did I get this old? Why couldn't I find my soulmate? What was wrong with me? Was I not lovable? I simply wasn't coping.

Begging the universe to be kind to me, I desperately wanted time and space to meet a decent man, get to know him properly, fall in love, and make sure we were compatible before committing my womb and my life to him. *Please, universe, I just need time.*

And then it came to me. I had an epiphany. Why hadn't I thought of this earlier? I would freeze my eggs. Wow, I was a genius! What a perfect solution: put my eggs on ice and safely store them, as an insurance plan, until I hooked up with my Mr Right. Conserve the little fertility I had left—that was the answer.

A massive smile came across my face. How clever was I? Optimism and relief surged through my veins. I was back in the game again.

Of course, I had no idea what was involved in the freezing process, but convinced it was possible, I scheduled a lunchtime appointment at the medical centre close to my office, deliberately requesting a female physician. Walking into the surgery, I checked in and sat down in the busy waiting area. I scoured the room, fascinated by the spectrum of patients around me, wondering what their stories were. And I had plenty of time to ponder. I waited and waited, my whole lunch hour spent. And then I heard it: my name being called. Excitedly, I hurried into the consulting room.

My lady doctor was lovely, perhaps a couple of years older than me. I began to open my mouth to tell my story. I felt an overwhelming urge to justify myself, to argue that *I really and truly have exhausted all avenues and efforts to find a man, but I'm getting too old now, and I want to have children. And I am really sorry that I failed this life mission, and I promise it's not my fault. So please, please, please, freeze some of my eggs …*

But I resisted the urge to go into detail. The Nazi at the front desk had insisted my appointment was time-restricted. Barely in the consulting room for thirty seconds, I quickly confessed my failure to find a man to father my children. And, given my age, I wanted to freeze my eggs.

"Sure," was the doctor's immediate supportive response. She didn't even blink an eye—no judgement, no negative comments or attempts to tell me I was wrong. "You will need to see a fertility specialist to talk about your options. Here is a referral to take with you." She then kindly gave me the details of a reputable fertility clinic in the city. After less than five minutes, I was politely ushered to the door.

Okay, that was surprisingly easy. Time to take the next step.

Finding a Clinic

I was elated. It looked like my insurance plan was going to come to fruition. Phew! I was about to buy myself some time. Driving home that afternoon, I was filled with a sense of hope and gratefulness. Time was of the essence. Eagerly, the following day, I picked up the phone and rang the fertility clinic.

My queries, however, were continually deflected. I soon found out that I couldn't just ring up the clinic to make an appointment. The clinic operated as a central hub, housing a multitude of various medical practitioners, including nurses, psychologists, and other paramedical staff. Linked to this central hub was a group of individual fertility specialists, including gynaecologists and obstetricians, some of whom had their own independent practises running from different premises.

First, I had to make a list of affiliated specialists; then I had to ring their respective receptionists one by one to find an available appointment. What I quickly found out was that if you needed assisted fertility services in this city, you were going to have to wait. Some doctors had a wait list several months long. Are you kidding me? My eggs were about to expire! I couldn't wait *months.*

Each phone conversation chipped away at my enthusiasm. Disappointment followed disappointment. My entire day was lost searching. I was starting to panic. I needed to calm my nerves down.

Impatiently, I started the process again the next day. I must have sounded distraught following the announcement of yet another fully booked calendar, as one very kind receptionist suggested I try a doctor who had only recently become affiliated with the central hub. He was located on the opposite side of the city, across the river. His name was not on my list. This was my break. What a lovely lady.

Quickly, I rang the new clinic, and they did indeed have availability. Yay! My appointment was ten days away. Thank you, universe! The insurance plan was in motion. I was going to get my happily-ever-after after all. Woo-hoo! I breathed a massive sigh of relief.

Appointment Day

The clinic was not within walking distance from my office, but it was close enough to step out of work for only an hour. Ensuring I had plenty of time to park, I drove to my appointment early.

Thrilled to be putting my insurance plan into action, I stepped into the art deco building. The reception room was modern, clean, and stylish. I approached the counter and registered my presence. With no one else waiting, I sat quietly, taking in my surroundings: a timber-panelled feature wall, pastel printed cushions, and healthy green plants. On the table was a scattering of women's health magazines, along with conception and pregnancy pamphlets available to read. Calmly I contemplated what lay ahead.

A deep voice interrupted my thoughts. My name was being called. I looked up to see a man with thick dark hair and glasses. With an authoritative voice, he again called my name. I was beckoned down the hall to his consulting room on the far right.

I entered the room and took a seat. This wasn't an ordinary consulting room. It was also modern, with stark white walls and brightly coloured décor. The furniture was arranged very differently to the old-school doctor-patient setup. With a small coffee table separating us, the ambience was peaceful.

Unlike my experience with general-practitioner appointments, where I had mere minutes to vomit a diatribe of symptoms to a physician I had never met, I didn't feel any sense of urgency. Sitting relaxed, the doctor in front of me—my now adopted gynaecologist—began to speak in a deep comforting voice with a distinct Kiwi accent. I trusted him immediately.

I began by explaining and justifying my situation: my age, my failure to find a partner to bear children with, and my desire to buy some time to continue my search for the right man, settle down, and make babies together. And then, of course, live happily ever after.

He was very professional and informative. My dilemma, as I described it, did not make him flinch. Like it was a normal everyday request, he began to explain all the factors I should consider in making an informed decision.

To ensure my reproductive system was intact, I accompanied the doctor to his adjoining surgery room. In the middle of the room was a gynaecological examination chair—a high-set chair with stirrups for easy access. Using a device shaped like a microphone, the doctor viewed my internal organs to assess if I was healthy. I had no complications. My womb was good to go.

We ventured back into the consulting room for a chat. And out came the statistics.

The Facts

I love knowledge, and I love being treated like an intelligent woman. I like detail and theory, and I have respect for professionals who recognise this. The facts, which I craved, were being laid out in front of me.

I will never forget the graph: a fertility graph that plotted a women's probability of falling pregnant against her age. It visually represented, right in front of me, my chances of motherhood sliding off a cliff.

If I was reading this correctly, I had a 14 per cent chance of conception at age thirty-seven, which would drop down to 8 per cent by the age of thirty-nine. Woah! Panic struck and I could barely breathe. *Deep breaths … deep breaths,* I reminded myself. This was useful, albeit terrifying, information. *It's okay,* I told myself. *I am going to circumvent the odds.*

Interestingly, the doctor casually mentioned that, unfortunately, watching celebrities have children late in life can be misleading. He went on to explain that a small percentage of women are under- or over-fertile and don't reflect the graph. And women having babies into their late forties are likely using egg donation. So don't be complacent, he told me. Wow, harsh advice.

Following the reality check of my declining fertility, the doctor proceeded to describe the freezing process. The egg, I was told, is the biggest cell in the body. Due to its size, it crystalizes once frozen, diminishing the quality of the cryopreserved egg. The likelihood of a frozen egg leading to a live birth, a baby, is around 7 per cent.

What? 7 per cent! A single digit? Holy crap! If I thought I was panicking before, now I was almost suffocating. Under no circumstances did 7 per cent constitute an insurance plan!

I began to do the maths in my head. I had roughly a one-in-fourteen probability of success. Taking this literally, I would need to freeze fourteen eggs, undergo fourteen embryo transplants, and experience thirteen failed pregnancies. After which, I should get a live birth. Statistically speaking …

Now, if I assumed a three-month cycle for each failed pregnancy attempt (probably unrealistic, but I needed a figure for my equation) and then a nine-month gestation period, it could take me over four years to get one baby. Four years to potentially get one baby! On top of that, I still needed to find Mr. Right, fall in love, and decide to create a family together. That could take another year or more! Holy cow, that could all take five years! ... I was suddenly very sad.

I need to point out in writing this memoir that I acknowledge there have been several technological advances in assisted reproductive treatments of late, with higher success rates available now for cryopreserved eggs. However, this was 2010, and this was my reality.

The Suggestion

After deflating my aspirations, the doctor remained upbeat. He had another option in store. He continued to tell me that a frozen embryo, however, had a 37 per cent chance of creating a baby. Better than one-in-three odds. Freezing an embryo was the more viable option.

Hmm ... That was interesting, but how was I going to get an embryo? I wasn't even in a relationship. Acknowledging that I came in to investigate the possibility of freezing my eggs for use with a future partner, he explained that I could use a sperm donor to create the embryo. A stranger, someone who I had never met, not my soulmate. What on earth was this doctor suggesting?

As a throwaway line, he made mention that he was sure there would be plenty of men out there who would gladly go down this path with me. If I met someone who already had children of his own, he might support the idea of me having a baby using my frozen embryo.

Let me get this right. This charming doctor, this respectable man, was suggesting that I could find a partner who would be happy for me to get pregnant with someone else's child? This was a lot to digest. And I wasn't entirely convinced. It was an uplifting concept, but I got the impression that this doctor was wearing rose-coloured glasses. I couldn't even find a man who was willing to settle down and bear his own children with me, let alone someone else's.

I reminded myself that I came in here to freeze my eggs, my *unfertilised* eggs, not have some random's baby.

Single-Mother Option

With all the evidence in front of me, the doctor then asked, "Would you consider having a baby on your own?"

What? What the heck was he talking about?

Given my age and my healthy reproductive system, he saw no reason why I couldn't get pregnant now, have a baby now, and find the love of my life later on. *Excuse me? Ah, no.*

No, I had never considered the idea of having a child on my own. And no, I had no ambition to become a single mother. What was this doctor trying to tell me? I thought he just said I could easily find a man to share my frozen embryo with. Was he now suggesting he didn't hold much hope of me finding such a man?

I'm sure these thoughts never entered his head. I was being irrational. He was professional and was clearly trying to detail options with the highest chance of success.

Although I was taken aback, it did get me thinking. Never had I given thought to the notion of *not* meeting my soulmate, *not* finding *the one* to have children with. Admittedly, I felt frustrated and exhausted, and hope was wearing thin. But even in my darkest hours, I had never given up the dream of my happily-ever-after. And I never questioned the sequence of meeting *the one* and then settling down to have children.

I was rattled by the doctor's suggestion. This was the first time in my life I had been presented with a second option, an alternative life plan, an option that took away the need for my soulmate ... well, at least in the interim. This single mother option certainly had merits. I just wasn't ready to digest it.

In closing, the lovely doctor handed me pamphlets outlining online forums and websites for women choosing to go down the single-mother path. He then stepped me through the pricing structure. I politely thanked him and walked out the door.

I found the experience extraordinarily informative and very confronting. I had just been told my chances of having a baby were about to fall off a cliff, the prospect of freezing my eggs had only a 7 per cent success rate, and due to my age, perhaps I should give serious consideration to becoming a single mum. That was a lot to take in!

It was nice to find out that I had more than one option, but I didn't aspire to have a stranger's baby. I just wanted to buy myself some time. And sadly, 7 per cent odds were not an insurance plan.

As much as I wanted to be a mum, I wanted to create my family with my soulmate. I wanted the complete package. I wasn't willing to give up my happily-ever-after just yet. Thanks, but no thanks!

CHAPTER 15

The Last Straw

With no insurance plan, suffering from SWC35+, and a loudly ticking time bomb, I was running out of ideas. Weeks off thirty-seven, my life plan looked grim.

Life Plan #8

1. Find my soulmate and fall in love by 37 ½
2. Get pregnant within 12 months
3. Have my first child at 39
4. Have my second child at 40
5. Get married at 41
6. Live happily ever after.

I had no wing-woman, no time, and no prospects. Reluctantly, I had to start internet dating—immediately!

eHarmony

I had always rejected the idea of shopping online for my soulmate. To me, it was the opposite of serendipity. Yes, I wanted my Mr. Right, but I was fixated on the universe putting us together in a romantic, fleeting moment. Our eyes would meet, my heart would pound, my breath would shorten, and I would know. Spending money to sift through thousands of online dating profiles fell far short of a chance meeting. No fairy tale required the damsel in distress to pour through a dozen internet sites to get her prince. Rapunzel didn't have access to wifi, Cinderella couldn't afford a computer, and Sleeping Beauty—well, she was asleep. No, the fairy tales taught me that my prince would cross my path incidentally.

But this was my last straw. I had to throw serendipity out the window.

Now, to apply a little perspective, internet dating may be prevalent nowadays, but a decade ago, in my circle of friends, it was not the norm. Only one of my close friends, Brenda, had entered the online dating world, and I was scarred from her horror stories.

Brenda recalled some colourful experiences—and they weren't all pretty colours. She warned me to be wary and wasn't convinced I had the backbone to survive the dating antics. She cautioned me to throw away romanticism and never assume exclusivity. Unless a man removes his online profile, assume he is simultaneously dating other women. It sounded gruesome.

I couldn't afford hang-ups, however. I had to break down my barriers. I had to start shopping!

Brenda recommended eHarmony. Apparently, this site was less known for random hook-ups. She helped me with my profile, and immediately, I started getting matches for consideration. Who would have thought it would be this quick?

I culled my potentials down to two and made contact. Candidate one had a great smile and a professional appearance, whilst candidate two was a younger prospect with a friendly face. Email exchanges ensued.

A front runner was emerging. Captivated by candidate one's wit and written expression, I hastily chose to focus my energy on just one egg. Juggling men was definitely not in my comfort zone.

Over the next few weeks, Gary and I spent hours transcribing our lives in a frenzy of email dialogue. He lived far south, in Victoria, but his work took him to Brisbane for weeks at a time. And he saw himself moving there in the future. Our apparent compatibility seemed endless: our identical tastes in music, our dedication to our careers, our day-to-day life, our desire to travel … tick, tick, tick, tick. On paper, he was perfect.

The Towel Story

Too much time had passed. I was getting invested, and we hadn't even laid eyes on each other. We had to meet. Gary was due in Brisbane the following week, so he booked dinner at an award-winning Indian restaurant in Fortitude Valley.

D-day arrived. Buzzing with excitement and anticipation, I spent hours pruning and preening and getting myself glamorous. I hopped in my car, music blaring, and drove to meet my date. It was really happening!

I parked the car and walked across the street. Gary had agreed to meet me at the bar. Stepping through the door, I scanned the room. At first glance, I couldn't find him. I immediately panicked. What if he stood me up? The thought hadn't entered my head until now.

I looked again. Hmm … I could see a man on his own, perched on a stool beside a bar table. But he didn't look right. Feeling awkward, I stood still in the doorway.

The man at the bar table beckoned me over. Oh, dear! It was him. *What?* He barely resembled his obviously Photoshopped profile picture. *Oh no!*

Aghast, I didn't know what to do. My smile disappeared, and my enthusiasm evaporated. Gary looked at least ten years older than his photo. My heart began to race for all the wrong reasons. I reluctantly walked over to greet him. I don't remember being polite. I'm sure I was. Inside my head, I was screaming, *Oh my God, what am I doing?*

I reconciled that this was my first-ever internet dating introduction. I just wasn't used to this feeling. Maybe it was nerves? Perhaps this is normal? Or was it my sixth sense telling me to run? My first impression, however, was a definite fail.

My novice approach to dating online was evident. Foolishly, I had agreed to have dinner. Bad mistake! I wanted to leave, but Gary had made a significant effort, so I couldn't walk out. That would be rude. *Do unto others as you would have them do unto you,* I reminded myself of what Aunty used to tell me. I would be gutted if someone walked out on me. I had to be civilised and honour my agreement. I said I would have dinner, so I had to toughen up. What harm was there? At least I knew the food would be great.

The conversation flowed. Although with my reputation for talking nonstop, I shouldn't have been surprised by this. Gary commented on my initial reaction and presumed that I was nervous. Perhaps I was. The meal was, as expected, delicious.

Exchanging courtesies after dinner, we each went on our way. I needed to digest the events and immediately rang Zoe. She calmed me down, and we both agreed I was likely overwhelmed. Perhaps I needed to give him another chance.

On our second date, Gary took me to a local winery for a gourmet lunch. My doubts crept in again. I couldn't put my finger on it. Clearly, we enjoyed the same lifestyle. Perhaps I was being unfair. This man did seem genuinely interested in me and could hold a decent conversation. Maybe my sixth sense was wrong?

By now, I had invested two months of my precious time. Our goals seemed aligned. And Gary was keen to take things further.

Noticing my reluctance, Gary offered me a carrot: a clincher to seal the deal. He offered to accompany me to the FIFA World Cup in South Africa. Knowing I held two tickets, and knowing I was looking for a travel companion, he promptly offered his services. How could I pass up a man who shared my love of travel? My arm was twisted, and the deal was done. I decided to give Gary a chance.

Long-distance relationships were my forte, although not by choice. Appreciating the effort required to make it work, I booked my flights to spend time with Gary in his home environment. I was eager to have some fun.

I arrived at his house during office hours, so he had left a key under a plant for me to gain access. A relatively new construction, his home was clean and adequately furnished. Everything appeared in order. Time to relax and have a shower. I just needed a towel.

Texting back and forth, I asked Gary where to find a towel. He promptly replied, "The towels are in the linen cupboard, next to the dining room." Great! Off I went.

I opened the cupboard: no towels. Like, zero towels. Fine. A minor issue. So I wandered around the house to find where they might be. And then I kept wandering … and wandering. I found one towel hanging above the bathtub, but it looked used. I wanted a clean towel. No bother; they had to be somewhere.

I texted again, just in case I had missed a location. Gary sternly responded that the towels were in the linen cupboard as described.

Ooh, that was a bit weird. Maybe he was busy at work, and my texts were a nuisance. I decided to delay the shower. I would just chill out until he got home.

But my curiosity got the better of me. I rechecked the linen cupboard. The shelves were empty. I was not going nutty. I continued to turn the house upside down, and then—I found them. Yay! The ominous towels were hiding in the washing machine. That made sense. Gary mentioned his cleaner was at the house earlier in the day. A full load of wet towels remained in the machine. She had forgotten to hang them on the clothesline.

With the mystery solved, I read my book while I waited for Gary's arrival.

I enjoyed a glass of red wine while Gary cooked our dinner— tender steak, steamed vegetables, and mushroom sauce, very tasty. After which, he presented me with a folded dry towel. "Oh, where did you find that?" I enquired.

"In the linen cupboard, exactly where I told you they were," he replied in a condescending voice. What?

I didn't say a word. I casually walked into the bathroom to find the dirty towel hanging above the bathtub had been removed. I opened my folded towel, and yes, it was indeed the same dirty towel that had been hanging on the railing.

Was this guy for real? I was gobsmacked. Who lies over a towel?

Appreciating I was a guest, I restrained my outrage, and instead I calmly asked, "Is this towel the one that was hanging up in the bathroom?"

Oh, dear! It was like a red rag to a bull. Gary was off! He was mad. He was caught in a lie and was not backing down. Adamant it came from the cupboard, he flung obscenities, suggested I was delusional, and scolded me for calling him a liar.

What the heck? Who really cares about the location of a towel? Why did it matter? Just man-up and say, "Sorry, the towels weren't in the cupboard." But no. He simply couldn't admit he was wrong, even over such a minor thing.

What thought processes must have gone through his head? It was obvious I knew the cupboard was empty. A blind man could have figured that out. What did he hope to achieve by holding onto his story? He must have known such antics would lose my respect.

What a twat!

It wasn't the first time he had fabricated the truth. When booking our flights to South Africa, he had to admit he distorted his age on his eHarmony profile. There was no way around it; his birthdate was in front of me, right there in black and white. With his tail between his legs, he conceded he wanted to fall into a lower age bracket to attract younger women.

Evidently, honesty wasn't one of his strong suits. And neither was the art of apology; as neither was forthcoming. This home visit was off to a real treat—not!

A few weeks along, Gary booked a weekend getaway to Queensland's Sunshine Coast. Zoe and her partner, George, were joining us. I was excited to share some experiences together as couples.

I love the Sunny Coast, as it is affectionately called. A couple of years earlier, my brother lived on the canals at Mooloolaba overlooking the Glass House Mountains. Bro would take me on bushwalks to hidden waterfalls and drive me around the coast as my personal tour guide. My brother has a knack for finding remote and interesting places to explore. Returning to the Sunny Coast and reminiscing about my time with Bro made me smile.

Once we had checked in, Gary was fixated on taking the four of us to the Sunshine Coast Hinterland to find a cheese factory he had once visited. Happy to go with the flow, we all hopped in the car for the forty-five-minute drive. Back then I didn't own a smart phone with a navigation app, but Gary assured us he knew where he was going, so Zoe, George, and I were content to talk and laugh and take in the scenery.

Time was getting on, and we were all getting hungry. Our forty-five-minute trip was now at two hours. "We're nearly there," we kept getting told.

"Are you sure you know where you're going?" Zoe asked with impatience. And that comment was enough to hold us as prisoners. No one was going to get away with suggesting Gary was wrong.

At this stage, the three of us had had enough. Hostages now for three hours, we were begging to stop, anywhere, for food, any food. We needed to be fed. But Gary was in control of the car. He was on a personal mission, and we were trapped on the ride.

Until finally, there it was: a small, nondescript outbuilding with adjoining carpark. Nothing special. No tourist signage. And no customers to be seen. The infamous cheese factory. Gary parked the car, and finally, we were set free. Fresh air at last! What a nightmare!

We walked inside to find a small delicatessen with limited cold food choices. Unimpressed, Zoe and I stood our ground. We wanted lunch—a proper lunch. We felt we deserved it after sitting in the car for hours. We demanded Gary take us to another venue. Reluctantly he gave in and we eventually found a lovely little café in Montville and enjoyed a pleasant hot meal.

Gary's recollection of the cheese factory was entirely different from what we discovered. But it didn't matter; his arrogance was revolting. What a complete waste of time. No surprise, Zoe and George ventured out alone the next day.

Refusing to believe it took him three hours to find the cheese factory, the following morning, Gary hopped in the car and drove me back up the mountain. Making excuses for the previous day, he was going to convince me he knew how to get there—on his own, without a map. He didn't want my directions; that would defeat the purpose. He had to prove he was right. This time, he took a different route, approaching the mountain from the north.

So I spent another day trapped in the car with a man who couldn't take direction—getting lost, getting angry, blaming anything but himself, and of course, not reaching the final destination, that darn, bloody cheese factory! The man just couldn't admit he was wrong. What a pork chop!

My one attempt to assist with directions led him to point his finger straight in my face. Who does that? Pointing a finger is a serious misdemeanour in my books. It is an aggressive nonverbal expression of power and domination. I wasn't having a bar of it.

Why was I even in the car with this guy? Why was I calling him my boyfriend? How on earth was I going to travel to South Africa with him? I wanted out.

A week before our departure, I was walking with my mum deliberating my upcoming trip. Gary and I had hardly spoken since our Sunny Coast trip. Could I suffer through two weeks with him overseas? I really wasn't sure. His flights were booked, and as far as I knew, he was still turning up. Should I renege on my offer?

It was too late to find a replacement, and I did want a travel buddy. Even if we weren't intimate, surely we could at least enjoy the adventure together? Surely? It was the FIFA World Cup. How could it go wrong? I had travelled with male friends before; we just needed to be considerate of each other. That couldn't be too hard. My optimism won.

Arriving at the airport to check in, I realised I may have overestimated my tolerance levels. Standing at the desk, Gary began by demanding an aisle seat. Not asking for one, no—outright refusing to sit anywhere but the aisle. I'm sure the airline assistant must have been cursing him inside her head. Oh, dear, what had I done? Inflight entertainment is a glorious thing—getting to catch up on all the new-release movies. My mind was occupied for the entire twenty-four hours in the air, there was no need to interact with Gary.

Landing in Johannesburg, we collected our bags and strolled to get the hire car, which was booked in my name. But of course, Gary insisted he had to drive. Even though I had previously driven a vehicle across Europe and spent a year in Greece, my international driving skills were ignored.

After the additional paperwork and an hour standing at the counter, we eventually hopped in the car. It was quickly evident that Gary was not comfortable behind the wheel in this foreign country. As the passenger, I naturally assumed the role of navigator. Departing the hire car venue, perhaps a kilometre along the road, I dutifully instructed Gary to turn left at the traffic signals about three kilometres ahead. As we approached the intersection, I kindly reassured him this is where we needed to turn. "Turn left here."

"I know! I know!" he rudely proclaimed. Okay, this was now the third time he had refused directions. So, in addition to his inability to admit he was wrong and his inability to say he was sorry, I now added the inability to take instruction to Gary's blacklist. I sat quietly in the car. This guy was a complete waste of space.

Inside our first bed and breakfast, we had barely put our bags on the floor when Gary tried to turn on the television. Following three failed attempts, I picked up the phone and rang reception. Gary was pissed! The doorbell rang, and a kind gentleman entered the room to show us which buttons to press. Voila, the TV was on.

And so was Gary's rage. "How dare you say I can't turn on a television!" were just a few of the words that came out of his mouth.

Enough was enough. This guy was a Fruit Loop! I asked him to leave. I handed him his half of the World Cup tickets and told him to find somewhere else to stay. I reminded him that I had paid for everything, and it was all in my name. So he could go find a taxi and somewhere else to sleep.

"What?" he exclaimed. He appeared genuinely shocked that I had told him to leave. And he was clearly offended, as he threw a tantrum like a two-year-old child.

The tournament was being held across different cities, including Johannesburg, Durban, and Cape Town, to name a few. "You can't leave me on my own!" he demanded. It suddenly came out that Gary wasn't the well-travelled guru he made himself out to be. He was afraid to go solo and pleaded with me to stick with him.

I was taken aback. Surely he wanted to part company? Why else would he behave like such a tosser? Now that he was being put on the spot, I saw in front of me a wounded child—an intolerable wounded child, but suffering nonetheless. My better self agreed to stay with Gary for the remainder of the trip—as travel buddies only. To be fair, I knew it would have been impossible for him to find accommodation at this late notice. My pity prevailed.

The next two weeks were memorable. Not always fun, but there were some definite highlights. Apart from the ear-splitting favelas at each stadium, the soccer matches were brilliant. I was proud to be wearing green and gold, watching Australia. The atmosphere and the strangers I met along the way outweighed my Gary torture. His antics didn't stop, but I painstakingly held my tongue. And I ran into some Aussie friends. Six degrees of separation; it truly amazes me.

On the plane home, we each sat in our own aisle seat, more than five rows apart. Phew! I was finally free.

Gary, to be forever known as the Towel Guy, was thankfully out of my life for good. I had dodged a bullet. Imagine if I had been unfortunate enough to have children with him? The thought of waking up next to him in two years or more made me violently ill. I couldn't think of anything worse.

How did I stoop this low? How did I even rationalise in my head that Towel Guy was good enough to be considered a prospect for a life partner? There were moments when I permitted myself to believe (well, at least tried to convince myself) that I could be happy with Towel Guy for the rest of my life. Who was I kidding?

I had lowered my standards so insanely low because I desperately wanted to settle down and have children. The time bomb kept ticking in my head, reminding me *you don't have the luxury of time. If this one doesn't work, you won't get your happily-ever-after. The sums just don't add up.* It scared me to think how close I had come to a disaster.

Even though I was experiencing significant distress from my failing life plan, Towel Guy was *not* an option!

CHAPTER 16

The Decision

If Towel Guy reflected the quality of men left out there, then I was done. I quit! I couldn't put in any more energy. I was exhausted and emotionally depleted.

Officially, I had failed—failed society's expectations of me; failed to follow in Aunty and Uncle's footsteps; failed to find my Prince Charming, get married, have children; and failed to live happily ever after. I was left on the shelf, and I was completely crushed.

Swamped by self-doubt and sadness, I kept playing my life over in my head. *How did I get here? What did I do wrong? Were my expectations too high? Was I supposed to accept a dud? Did people lie to me about knowing when I had found the one? Why did it happen for others but not me? Wasn't I good enough?*

There were no answers to my questions. For twenty years, I had been holding onto a life plan I couldn't fulfil, a see-saw of anticipation and hope and a bucketload of tears. My happily-ever-after was gone to ruin.

True love had evaded me. My soulmate had never arrived ... or maybe he just didn't exist? There would be no more relationships, no more tears. I was destined to be single.

The only thing left to salvage now was motherhood. I was finally ready to consider the fertility doctor's suggestion, the *second option*, to have a child on my own. He had made the concept sound so normal.

Where to Begin?

Wracked, unfairly, with the negative connotations of single parenthood, I needed to get my head around the idea of becoming a solo mum. To be honest, having grown up mostly with a single mother, I never expected my life journey would follow suit. Watching my mum struggle with finances and loneliness, I wanted better for myself. It was hard to visualise this as an ideal outcome.

I had a lot of doubts. Was having a child on my own selfish? How would my son or daughter feel about not having two parents? Was I submitting him or her to a life of adversity?

Growing up, I had struggled with the stigma of being the child of a single parent. It wasn't common back then, at least not in our circle of friends. I never missed having a dad. I had other male role models who loved me, especially Uncle, whom I lived with for my teenage years. But I didn't enjoy being interrogated about my family situation. My own school friends couldn't have cared less about my parents, but adults, on the other hand, could be rude.

So how was I different? How was this second option different? For one thing, it was 2010. The divorce rate had escalated, and families now came in all shapes and sizes. It was a new century, with new ways of being and more freedom and choices than ever before.

My mother never planned to become a single mum. My father passed away when I was almost nine. Single life was not her intention. Similarly, many women don't choose the path of solo motherhood. It happens incidentally, and they just have to adjust.

I needed to be real, and I needed to apply perspective. I wasn't following my mother's path: I went to university, the first in my family. I was a qualified civil engineer with a glowing career. On my own, I had travelled overseas and purchased property. Without aspiring to, I had learnt to be independent.

I suddenly realised I was carving out my own path, not following in anyone else's footsteps and not following anyone else's rules. I was healthy. My womb was good to go, and I longed to be a mum. Whatever the outcome, I knew any child of mine would be wanted and loved.

I started my online due diligence.

Online Communities

Scouring the internet, I was pleasantly surprised by the extent of information available on becoming a solo mother by choice—an SMC, with websites and forums from many countries dedicated to the topic. I discovered that many women from across the globe had relayed their plights, their wins, and their hurdles in becoming an SMC. It was reassuring.

It became apparent that I wasn't alone, and this wasn't a new phenomenon. Hundreds, if not thousands, of single women from all walks of life, for a multitude of reasons, had pioneered this journey before me. There was another world out there.

Inspired by these women, I was becoming more and more motivated. I joined a few different forums and began reading through pages of information threads. There was no stone left unturned. Every question or topic, from every angle, had been discussed and explored. I had found a gold mine.

I was surprised to find that each state in Australia had different laws attached to the use of donor sperm. I was grateful to be living in

Queensland, which housed one of the most reputable fertility clinics in Australia. I felt reassured.

I found myself interrogating different websites daily. There was so much information to glean, and I was fascinated by all the stories. It was painful reading about women who left it too late, who couldn't forgo the notion of bearing children with their Mr. Right. They held on too long to a broken dream, and sadly, their eggs expired.

Financial fears were also genuine. And fair enough: raising a child is expensive. It was nice to see some innovative ideas and encouragement. And there were ideas on how to tackle the "no father" issue. From procedures to parenting, laid out in front of me was a wealth of knowledge. The websites and forums became my haven, my safe place where I felt connected to other women in a parallel universe.

Decision Time

I was beginning to embrace the concept of single motherhood fully. My courage was building, and I was almost convinced I could pull this off. But there were a few little hurdles to jump.

My niggling doubts were centred around other people's opinions, not my own. What would others think of this path? Why was I worrying so much about what other people thought? I was putting so much pressure on myself to please those around me when what was at stake was my lifetime of happiness. Why did I care so much about fitting in and following society's one-option plan?

How I chose to live my life shouldn't matter. It was my life journey, and I had to play the cards I was dealt—my cards, in my hand. I shouldn't be making decisions based on anyone else's expectations of me or women in general.

Be brave, I told myself. *Don't let the little voice inside your head destroy your chance of motherhood.* I wanted to become a mum. And I had an opportunity sitting right in front of me.

I took solace from the hundreds of other single women around the world going through a comparable journey—different, but the same. I had so much respect for the SMCs and SMC hopefuls who were actively pursuing their dream of motherhood.

It was incredibly hard coming to terms with the fact that I wasn't making a family with my soulmate. But I had to act now. I kept picturing the fertility graph—that graph of horror!

I began to reconcile that I could find a man, Mr. Right, later in life, but I wouldn't be able to have biological children. I had to sacrifice my dream of meeting my soulmate now in order to fulfil my dream of becoming a mum.

Statistically, almost 50 per cent of marriages ended in divorce, meaning 50 per cent of people aren't getting their happily-ever-after. It wasn't just me. I just hadn't made it past the starting line. I had failed to launch.

But the statistics also meant that more single men would be entering the market as their marriages failed. There would always be a new stream of divorced men out there to find and sample. Maybe I could get my happily-ever-after after all? Perhaps I just needed to swap the order? I could aspire to be a stepmother—not an evil one, of course—and find happiness in a blended family.

My decision was made—I was going to take control of my destiny. My priorities would have to get reordered, as I needed to forge ahead alone. I was choosing the path to single motherhood.

A massive wave of relief swept over me. I could breathe easily. I could now move forward with the next goal. Life was, once again, optimistic. I was going to have a child before I reached forty.

CHAPTER 17

Taking Action

Watching friends struggle to fall pregnant in their mid-thirties was heartbreaking. At thirty-seven, I knew the road ahead might be an uphill battle. I didn't want to give myself any false expectations. I was touched by stories of women fighting for years to get pregnant to no avail—women who bravely tried time and time again to fulfil their dream of having a baby only to suffer unimaginable loss with each traumatic miscarriage. I couldn't comprehend the magnitude of their grief.

Wary of what lay ahead, I braced myself for the impending challenge. I picked up the phone and rang the clinic to make an appointment. The following week, I stepped once again into the familiar reception room with its modern décor. A smile came across my face as I breathed a sigh of relief. I'd been here before. I knew what to do.

Closing my eyes, I sat against the pastel-coloured cushions and reflected on the past eight months and how far I had come. The last time I was in this waiting room, my mind had been focussed on only one thing: finding my soulmate. I was obsessed with fulfilling my life plan. I was in a state of panic. All I could think about was men.

And yet, at this moment, with the blessing of time, I sat subdued and peaceful. Ironically, the last thing in the world I wanted right now was a boyfriend. I felt free.

My thoughts were interrupted—my name was being called by that soothing Kiwi voice. Walking down the hallway, I felt empowered. Once again, the lovely doctor put me at ease.

"I came to see you eight months ago to explore freezing my eggs," I began, "but instead, you suggested I consider having a baby on my own. Well … I have decided I want to do this. I want to have a baby now."

Nonchalantly, he proceeded to put together an action plan for pregnancy, appearing to be months in the making, before I abruptly interrupted. "I was hoping I could start this process straight away," I told him. "Like … today?"

"Oh!" he responded, and without a flinch, replied, "Okay. Let's get you up on the chair."

Intrauterine Insemination

With my feet in stirrups, I felt strangely comfortable conversing with the doctor whilst he was scanning my uterus internally. Watching the monitor, I could see a black-and-white image of my reproductive organs, my ovaries, my eggs. Thankfully, the scans showed a healthy ovarian cycle with a good-sized leading egg. Brilliant!

Based on my results, he suggested we (as in he and I) should do a round of intrauterine insemination (IUI). To explain this in laymen's terms, as I understood it, it meant that I would continue my natural menstrual cycle without any drugs. Then when my egg was about to be released down my fallopian tubes, as would happen in a regular monthly period, I would be inseminated with my chosen sperm.

The sperm would be deposited directly into my uterus (avoiding my vagina and cervix) using a needle the size of a joisting stick … okay, perhaps a little exaggeration. And to make sure the timing was accurate, I would have to inject myself with a smaller needle the night before to make sure my egg was released at the right time—simple! Now, I'm not a health professional, but this was how I explained the process to those who asked.

The IUI procedure was apparently suitable for healthy fertile women. Still, due to my age, the doctor decided we would try two cycles of IUI, and if we didn't get any success, we would revert to intravenous fertilisation (IVF).

Okay—that all seemed to compute in my brain. I didn't hear any concern in the doctor's voice. In fact, it was the opposite. Smiling from ear to ear, I could hardly contain my excitement. *Yay!*

Back in the consultation room, the doctor sat me down to describe the process I needed to follow. First, I needed to see a clinic nurse, then choose my donor, then see a counsellor, all within the next couple of days to qualify for this month's cycle. Fortunately, all the services were available under one roof on the opposite side of the city. Within an hour of walking out the door, I had all three appointments booked.

Choosing a Donor

The nurse called me into a private room. Warm and welcoming, with a comforting smile, her role was to walk me through the details of my upcoming procedure and answer any questions. Everything was on track. I then returned to sit in the waiting room. One consult down, two to go.

I began to feel butterflies in my stomach, and my heart started beating faster. I was about to meet the sperm lady—the clinician whose job was to administer the donor-sperm process. This was the consultation that made me nervous. I was about to choose the biological father of my child. Who would I choose to procreate with? The enormity of the decision that lay before me was incomprehensible. This was possibly the most important decision of my entire life.

Equipped with my yellow highlighter pen, I stood up and shook the sperm lady's hand as she led me into her office. With a professional approach, she asked me what features I was looking for in a donor. If I wasn't paying attention, I could have mistaken the experience for buying a new car—except that this purchase was lifelong. There would be no trade-ins, no future upgrades. This was a forever purchase. I had to make sure I wasn't buying a lemon.

It was at this stage that she told me each vial of sperm would cost nearly $1,000. Whoa … $1,000 for a teaspoon of semen! This had better be some good-quality produce!

I was handed a printout of profiles of all the donors with offerings being held on ice that month. They fell into two categories: Australian donors and international donors. At the time, in Australia, all sperm donations had to be classified as *identity release* (or *disclosed*), meaning the donor had to agree to have his details released once the donor-conceived child reached the age of eighteen if the child wished to seek the information. I was pleasantly surprised by this policy and found it comforting. I was also relieved to hear that the international sperm on offer came from a reputable sperm bank in America—a bank that had stringent screening processes to ensure the highest-quality candidates.

Presented with printouts from both donor categories, I found the contrast in information extreme. The local profiles were two pages in length without a photo. In comparison, the American profiles included an eight-page bio describing the donor and his features, along with his and his family's medical history, all supported by two photos, one as an adult and one as a baby.

Upon instruction from my gynaecologist, I immediately ditched the local donors. Our Australian sperm, as it turned out, was far inferior to the screened high-quality American sperm. "Does that mean our Australian men are duds?" I asked in jest. It turned out we don't pay donors in Australia; donations are made out of kindness and generosity of heart. In the US, however, candidates are paid for their high-potency, high-motility sperm.

As I would be undergoing an IUI, I needed to choose the better product to give me the highest probability of success. There would be no petri dish party. The sperm had to survive on their own in the harsh environment of my womb and fight their way to my egg. I had to pick good, strong swimmers, and lots of them. It was a natural insemination (as natural as you can get with a foot-long needle inserted into your vagina), so I had to stack the odds in my favour. An American donor it would be.

With my yellow highlighter in hand, I read through each profile; no ... no ... nope ... definitely not. I knew what I wanted: brown hair, fair skin, recessive coloured eyes, and O blood group. That was all. And why? vanity—pure and simple vanity. I wanted my child to look like me. And for medical reasons, I wanted the same blood type. I wasn't looking for an aeronautical engineer. I figured I had that covered.

Within minutes, I found a candidate who nearly fitted the bill. He had a sweet smile, but he also had brown eyes. He was definitely on the shortlist, though. I sifted through some more, marking all the compatible features on each printout.

And then I found him. My heart started racing. Not only did donor BJL tick all my boxes, but he had also written a considered and thoughtful synopsis of why he chose to become a donor. My heart melted. This man seemed so sincere. But even better—this man liked eighties music! What? He was perfect!

Unhesitatingly, I knew. I just knew! Every inch of my body was in alignment. Donor BJL was *the one*. I reread his profile, and he seemed too good to be true. My heart skipped a beat. I could hardly breathe. A wave of euphoria swept over me. I had found *the one*. The right one. Not my soulmate or Mr. Right, but the one I was going to make a baby with. I was 100 per cent convinced. There was not a doubt in my mind.

I finally experienced the feeling that had eluded me for so many years. I now understood what people meant when they told me, "You just know."

On cloud nine, I floated into the counsellor's room. In front of me sat a quirky middle-aged man, pragmatic in his approach. Expecting to be interrogated, I had prepared an array of responses to justify my sanity, validate my financial stability, and reassure my legitimacy to pursue this single-mother-by-choice pathway. I was armed and ready to battle.

But the questions were never fired. There was no test to pass. I was not being audited. *What? So I didn't have to prove myself?* Instead of a challenge, I was offered a wealth of information about how to navigate the possible issues I might face with a donor-conceived child—a child without a father. And what marvellous and supportive words of wisdom he offered.

He recommended I approach the situation in a similar manner to adoption, purporting that research indicates being open and telling children when they are young will likely eliminate trust issues. He also made a point of recommending I always use the term *donor*, not *dad*. He explained that if I refer to the donor as a dad, there is a chance my child could develop abandonment issues. Using the word *donor* removes any expectations associated with the word *dad*. Great advice.

The counsellor also talked about how other single mothers chose to tell their children about their conception. Some reasoned to their child, "We haven't found a dad yet, but together we can find one." The concept I loved the most, however, was the seed story, explaining that "Mummy bought a seed and planted it in her belly, and it grew into a baby, which is you." I really liked that story. It made me smile.

I was given references and book recommendations and walked away feeling confident that I could do this. It was all going to be okay.

CHAPTER 18

My Precious Cargo

Living close to work was convenient—a little too convenient. As a contractor, I could choose my start and finish times. And, more often than not, I was gently nudged into staying back late to help the team with the demanding workload. Up until now, it had been a win-win. I was paid for the extra hours, and the projects were finished ahead of schedule, making the boss look good. I'd had no other demands on my time. Zoe was no longer around to play with following her move three hours south to live with her boyfriend. Work kept me away from boredom and buffered my bank account.

But now, my focus was changing. I wanted to get pregnant and have a baby. I needed to start creating space in my life if I wanted to experience motherhood. Working five days a week till late in the evenings would never cut it. It was time for an adjustment.

The universe presented a solution. I snapped up an opportunity to move to the Gold Coast, into an apartment overlooking the Broadwater, across the road from a children's playground and a ten-minute walk to a shopping centre. It was perfect. With an hour's drive to the office, my temptation to work long hours was eliminated. My focus was redirected. It wasn't about money anymore; it was about lifestyle. I successfully negotiated a deal to work from home two days per week. I was looking forward to having time to myself to enjoy my new home and get acquainted with my new surroundings. Unpacking my boxes, however, would have to wait. I was due to get impregnated.

Insemination Day

It was almost time. I opened the fridge and there, on the top shelf, was the box with my pharmacy-dispatched medication to trigger ovulation, contained within a syringe that I would need to administer myself.

I pulled out the needle and read the instructions. And then I reread them, just to be sure. I told myself not to think about what I was about to do. "Don't think, just do"—another quote my aunt used to say when it was time for me to wash up the dishes. I pulled up my T-shirt to expose the skin on my stomach and then took a deep breath. As I breathed out slowly, I frantically stabbed myself and pushed down the plunger. In a split second, it was done. *Ha. I did it, I actually did it.* Incredibly pleased with myself, I let out a little chuckle.

I awoke the next day to the sound of rain. Oh, no! Rain always caused traffic delays. My one-hour drive could be doubled with lousy weather and peak-hour traffic. I madly showered and hopped in the car. My appointment with my gynaecologist was at nine o'clock. But first, I had to pick up my frozen sperm.

The rain was heavy; with my windscreen wipers on full throttle, I could hardly see the cars ahead of me. Panic was setting in. I wanted to cry. Today was insemination day. I tried to be calm and composed. My mind was racing at a hundred miles an hour. What if I didn't make my appointment? How much time did I have now that my egg was released? Why was there so much traffic on the road this early in the morning?

Arriving at the fertility clinic headquarters, I noticed an available parking space on the opposite side of the road. Without checking for vehicles, I hastily swerved across the concrete central median, avoiding the oncoming traffic, into the vacant space. Pulling in on an angle, I didn't even bother to straighten the car. The rain was pouring down, so I didn't waste time putting money into the parking meter. Surely there would be no inspectors out in this weather?

I opened the car door and made a dash across the road into the building. It was eight forty-five; I was fifteen minutes late. Considering the conditions, I had made good time.

The sperm lady greeted me at the reception desk and took me straight through to the storage room. In front of me was a metal container with a white translucent coating on its surface—the visible signs of dry ice. Opening the lid, she pulled out a sperm vial and read the label. "Is this the correct donor identification number?" she queried.

Wow, no room for error here. "Yes, that's the one," I responded.

She took the vial, wrapped it in a tissue, and asked me to put it under my bra strap in the middle of my chest. Yes, that is correct. My frozen sperm was nestled safely in between my boobs, ready for transportation to my next appointment. Apparently, my body temperature would assist in the thawing process, and where better to be harnessed than right on top of my heart?

It was like I was carrying a newborn baby. I was protecting that sperm with my life. With my hand shielding the vial, I hurried back to my car.

Driving across town, one hand on the steering wheel, one on my chest, I navigated the rain and the peak-hour traffic. For fifteen minutes, I couldn't stop thinking about my precious cargo. This time, parking was easy. And this time, I put money into the meter. I wasn't going to push my luck any further.

Smiling and relieved, I crossed the road to the clinic. After checking in, I sat down and breathed a massive sigh of relief. Stroking my vial of sperm, I couldn't contain my excitement.

The waiting was painful. Ten minutes felt like an hour. Where was my doctor? Why was he taking so long? Another ten minutes, and I was still sitting in the waiting room. What if my sperm got too hot? Should I take it out of my bra now? Please hurry up!

Finally, that familiar Kiwi voice called my name. This was it. I walked down the hallway. This time, I was taken straight to the stirrup-chair. I handed over my specimen, although the doctor didn't seem to caress the vial as lovingly as I did. In went the needle before I could register what was happening, and within seconds, the whole process was complete. And just like that, I was inseminated. I'd barely blinked an eye.

I stayed in the chair for a while as the doctor talked through my next steps. If a pregnancy test showed a positive result, I was to return in four weeks for a blood test. It was now a waiting game. I had to find some patience—a virtue I didn't possess. Zoe regularly insisted impatience was one of my failings.

Peeing on Sticks

Zoe may have been three hours away, but we spoke on the phone daily. And each day, I would check in. Against popular opinion, I started using pregnancy tests at the seven-day milestone. On no planet was I ever going to wait two weeks!

I opened the box and unwrapped the stick. The first morning pee was supposedly the best time to test. So I carefully angled the device and aimed. Then I gently placed the tester on the vanity. As expected, there was no line. I knew it was too soon, but I couldn't contain my eagerness.

I repeated this process each day. It was an expensive addiction. Having read other women's stories, I was well aware that my first attempt could fail. I knew the statistics, but I was trying not to focus on the negatives. I was torn. I wanted to believe this would work, hold on to faith, and not allow in any doubt. But I also felt the need to protect myself from heartbreak. It was a tough balancing act.

Each morning I held onto hope and anticipation as I peed on the stick. And then I rang Zoe for a debrief.

Eight sticks later, on a Saturday morning, I was heading off to start a three-day course on share trading and the stock market. Curiosity had led me to the course, which turned out to be incredibly insightful and informative about history and the world in general, not just trading. And I got to meet some fascinating people.

In a rush to get to my course, I was tempted not to bother with my morning ritual. But the packet was sitting within arm's reach, so I quickly ripped open the casing and positioned the stick, aimed, and left it on the bench whilst I hurriedly got dressed.

I returned five minutes later and checked the tester. I took a breath and then checked again. It looked suspiciously like a second line was forming. A faint pink line. It was questionable. I picked up the stick and put it up to the light bulb. *Hmm. I think it could be a line … maybe? Holy cow. Is it a line?* I immediately rang Zoe.

"It looks like a line!" I exclaimed. Zoe's excitement was parallel to mine. "I think I might be pregnant," I said and then let out a loud scream, as did Zoe. By now, the line was getting darker. It was definitely a line!

Oh my God, I was pregnant!

Given my age, many people would have recommended I withhold the information until a blood test confirmed my pregnancy and the risk of miscarriage was reduced at the end of the first trimester. But I'm not one to take advice readily. And being the world's most impatient woman, I couldn't keep my news to myself. I was too excited. I grabbed my bag, jumped in my car, and immediately rang my mum.

Standing in the foyer with a dozen other people waiting for the course to start, I felt smug. I felt invincible. I couldn't wipe the smile off my face.

The News

A blood test confirmed my prognosis. I was on my way to motherhood. Wow! I could hardly contain my elation.

People around me began to notice my change in demeanour. At around eight weeks pregnant, I opened the floodgates and confessed my newfound status to my workmates. Some of my colleagues knew I was single, but many did not. I didn't want to put myself into the uncomfortable position of having to answer questions about my partner (or lack thereof), so I chose to be blunt in delivering my news.

Speaking with confidence, I began by saying, "I am pregnant. And before you ask, I am single. I am thirty-seven and want to have a baby while I still can, so I have chosen to do this on my own." I wasn't seeking anyone's permission. I had made this decision and was owning it. People could be happy for me or not. It didn't matter.

I was prepared for some backlash. After all, I had technically failed in my life plan. I had failed to meet society's expectations of me. I had failed to find a father for my child. And I was bringing a child into this world knowing there would only be one parent. I wasn't sure what reactions I would get.

Surprisingly, I only got one negative response—to my face, anyway. It was from a religious man whose beliefs couldn't support the concept of procreation out of wedlock. And he wasn't comfortable that I appeared to be eliminating the need for a man. He felt that men's role in society was becoming diminished, and my actions were an example of this. Fair enough. He had his beliefs that served him. I, however, was pioneering my own beliefs to serve me. I acknowledged my colleague's concerns. But I had already painstakingly reconciled that I was creating a child who would have no father.

Of all the concerns I had about going solo, the notion of having a child without a dad to love and care for them plagued me the most. After my father passed, my mother never remarried. As the product of a single mother (not by choice), I think I fared okay. I was very lucky to have my uncle as my father figure, who I loved more than I could ever imagine. I also knew of friends whose biological fathers chose to abandon them, and they suffered long-term grief and resentment. I resolved that even if I had found a man to father my child, there was no guarantee he would stick around.

When I chose the SMC path, I made a conscious commitment to make sure my child would have male role models, by some means or another. I would just have to orchestrate it.

I was grateful I hadn't sought anyone's advice when making my decision. It was a deliberate move. No one else was walking in my shoes. No one close to me was following the path of a thirty-seven-year-old single woman, an SWC35+, desperate to become a mum before her eggs expired. What advice could others offer? They had no idea what I was going through.

Much well-intended advice had landed me a lot of heartache over the years and entrenched in me feelings of failure when I couldn't live up to others' expectations. So I didn't allow anyone to sway me from choosing the path of solo motherhood. I wasn't giving outsiders power over my life journey anymore. It was my life, my decision. And to my surprise, most people warmly embraced my position.

I was happy. In fact, I couldn't remember a time I felt happier.

CHAPTER 19

Pregnancy Alone

My temporary departure from the dating scene was refreshing. With my thoughts no longer focused on men, I could finally let down my armour. I could remove the facade that had covered the tracks of my tears, and I could stop pretending I wasn't lonely. After twenty years of chasing my life plan and stressing over something I had no control over, I could finally breathe and just be free.

My attention now was on the baby growing inside me and the life I wanted to create for us. *Us*—what a beautiful word. I closed my eyes and murmured *us*. It wasn't just me anymore. I was about to become part of a team, a team of two, mother and child, a family. My family! I couldn't believe how far I had come, and I couldn't wipe the grin off my face.

Geriatric Mother-to-Be

Confirmation of my pregnancy meant saying goodbye to my gynaecologist and starting a new relationship with an obstetrician. Following a promising six-week scan, I was referred to a local obstetrician on the Gold Coast. I was told I would need monthly check-ups to monitor the baby's and my progress, plus a series of antenatal scans and blood tests.

I arrived for my first appointment in plenty of time. The practice was located next to a private hospital, a ten-minute drive from home. Thankfully, the parking was easy and free. I walked into the tiny reception room—no modern décor like my fertility clinic, just enough chairs for a handful of patients and a polite unassuming lady behind the desk. There were no coloured cushions; in fact, there were no cushions at all, just old-fashioned metal-framed chairs with well-worn padding.

The doctor called me in, and I stepped into his room. "Hello," greeted a tall man with thinning dark hair wearing a plaid shirt. I didn't feel the same energy and vibe I'd experienced with the Kiwi doctor. I felt a little disappointed. Never mind; I wasn't there to make a friend.

Following the summation of my situation, I was ushered into the adjoining room, where I was asked to position myself upon the reclining chair. This time, the chair wasn't a stirrup chair. Yay! And this time, the examination was external. No more microphone cameras, thank goodness for that.

Lifting my shirt, the doctor painted my belly with translucent jelly. It felt wet and sticky. On the screen in front of me, I could see a two-dimensional black-and-white fuzzy image of my baby. Wow. My breath quickened. It was real.

"All the stats look fine," the doctor calmly advised. "There is only one baby, and the heartbeat is normal." I was given the green light. Hah ... I breathed a huge sigh of relief.

My obstetrician then walked me through the stages of pregnancy and what to expect. It was at this point that he raised concern over my age and the possibility of complications. Apparently, I was classified as a geriatric mother-to-be. That's right, at thirty-seven, I was labelled a geriatric! What? That seemed a bit harsh.

It was hard to concentrate after being labelled a fossil. The doctor asked me to think about a birth plan and whether I wanted a natural birth or caesarean. I was surprised to be offered the choice. I wasn't comfortable going under the knife—I felt there was an element of cheating—but I didn't want my baby put at risk. I needed to go home and take in all the information.

My Support Network

Moving to the Gold Coast was turning out to be a fantastic decision. I loved it there. The only downside was the distance from close friends and family. Maxine and Judy were ten hours south, along with my mum and brother. And Zoe was two hours and forty-five minutes away—if I kept to the speed limit.

This meant I didn't have anyone to accompany me to my appointments. Surprisingly, it didn't bother me. I was so absorbed in my growing baby, I was okay taking this journey on my own. My daily debriefs on the phone to Zoe made me forget I was geographically isolated. Between my work and pregnancy, I was kept fully occupied. Loneliness was a thing of the past. I was too excited thinking about the life I was about to live to be down on myself.

I chose to maintain my connection to some of the single-mother forums. I was reassured knowing hundreds of like-minded women were travelling a similar path. It's weird to think that these online communities made me feel safe and included. I never felt alone, nor did I feel different or that I was doing anything out of the norm.

At times, I would experience short bouts of panic. *Will I be a good mum? Can I do this? Can I afford this?* After each momentary lapse of reason, I would head back online and read dozens of inspiring stories of women succeeding against all the odds. It gave me hope.

The Revealing Scan

Reaching my second-trimester milestone was a relief, but I still had a few hurdles to jump. At thirteen weeks, I presented myself to an X-ray and imaging clinic that specialised in four-dimensional prenatal scans. I was about to have my nuchal translucency test to determine the risk of my baby having chromosomal abnormalities.

I sat in the waiting room and calmed myself for my impending scan. *Everything will be okay,* I told myself. *Whatever the result, I will deal with it. What will be will be.* I repeated these mantras over and over inside my head and took deep breaths.

As I waited, I noticed a row of plastic baby dolls above the counter. Half were dressed in pink T-shirts, the other half in blue. Huh? A wave of excitement began to rush through me. Would I be able to find out the sex of my baby? How exciting. I wanted one of those dolls!

My mind wandered to the list of baby names I was deliberating in my mind. My mum had already decided I was having a girl and had started crocheting pink blankets. I wasn't so sure. And I was undecided on a girl's name. A boy's name was easy: I would name him after my uncle, Nicholas. But Aunty's name was Beryl. Hmm ... yeah, not so sure about that. I had narrowed the girl's list to five names. I still had plenty of time to figure it out.

I was called as the next patient. As I walked into the room, I noticed the examination bed, lined with a paper towel.

"Lay down on the bed and raise your shirt," I was instructed. The practitioner, a friendly lady, probably in her twenties, began to describe the purpose of the ultrasound and what I should expect. She would measure the thickness at the back of the baby's neck.

"Can I find out the sex of my baby?" I eagerly asked.

Not wanting to get my hopes up, she replied, "Unfortunately we can't confirm the sex of the baby until the eighteen-week scan."

Never mind. I would just have to be patient.

Obediently, I raised my shirt while she slathered cold gooey gel onto my belly. As she glided a plastic transducer over my stomach, the image of my baby appeared on the screen in front of me. Perhaps a little alien-like, but beautiful nonetheless. I could see fingers and toes, a cute button nose, ears, eyelids, everything. I was in love! This adorable baby was wriggling around inside my belly, and I was watching every move. Bub was on display and made sure we knew it.

As the baby turned again, as if looking straight at me, legs bent and spreadeagled, I saw it. "What's that?" I exclaimed, pointing to the obvious appendage between the little legs.

The practitioner smiled. "Do you want to know the sex of your baby?"

"Of course!" I cried.

"You are having a boy. We don't often see the baby in a position where you can identify the sex this early. But it's pretty obvious."

I'm having a boy! It was a euphoric moment. I was having a boy. Absolutely perfect. My beautiful baby boy. I couldn't stop smiling.

The practitioner seemed happy with the ultrasound results. However, she advised me to take them to my obstetrician to discuss further. There was no need for any alarm at this stage.

I wiped the gunk off my belly and floated into the reception area to pay for the scan, which included a recording of the video on disk. I enquired about the cute little dolls on the shelf. I was told they were a replica size of an eighteen-week old baby and could be purchased with the scan. "A blue one, please," I requested.

Exiting the clinic on cloud nine, I immediately rang my mother. She needed to buy some blue wool!

At my follow-up visit, my obstetrician told me my calculated risk of Down syndrome was low, so I chose not to have an amniocentesis. Given my geriatric condition, it was recommended, but no thanks. There was no way I was having a needle inserted into my belly. My baby boy would be just fine.

Body Changes

Judy's three children were growing up fast, although I didn't get to see them often. I remembered clearly that each time Judy was pregnant, she complained about getting fat, feeling uncomfortable, and not enjoying the experience. I was prepared for the same fate. But it didn't happen. I absolutely loved being pregnant. I loved getting fat. I loved watching my belly grow. And I even reconciled that morning sickness was just nature's way of protecting the baby.

I was living the dream—fat and happy and eating the house down. Each day I would rub my belly and talk to my son. On the hour-long journey to work each day, I would play loud music and sing to him and tell him about my day. I hadn't even met him, yet he was already firmly cemented into my life.

Pregnancy appeared to agree with me. My cheeks were pink, and my skin felt great. My face glowed, and my hair was shiny. I was consistently happy.

Safety became my focus. I felt an overwhelming need to protect my unborn child and was filled with an enormous sense of responsibility. I had a new purpose: to safeguard my youngling. My motherly instincts had kicked in.

Experiencing pregnancy alone was not difficult, although I expected it to be. I was pleasantly surprised. There was no room for pity, no room for sorrow, no mourning over what could have been or the husband I couldn't find. No, this was a joyful time. I was filled with love for the baby growing inside me and optimism, hope, and anticipation for what lay ahead.

Passing the halfway mark was a wonderful feeling. My morning sickness was long gone, and now I was just left with cravings … for fast food. Tuesdays on my way home, I would take advantage of KFC's ten-dollar meal deal: six pieces of juicy fried chicken that melted in my mouth. That signature smell lingering in my car brought back memories of my teenage years hanging out with Maxine and Judy at our local KFC. I was also struggling to restrain myself from diverting into a McDonald's drive-through to pick up a Fillet-o-Fish on an almost daily basis.

It was not the ideal diet, and I cringe as I write this now. But I justified my indulgence as a pregnant disposition. *It's okay*, I told myself. *It's just a craving. I am balancing good food with bad.*

Well, the universe intervened. My geriatric condition was proving true. I developed gestational diabetes. Apparently, the disease is prevalent in older pregnant women. And I was one of those older women!

My diabetes led to ongoing check-ups at the nearby public hospital—and an end to my fast food binges. Out with the fried food, in with the vegetables. Paranoid about pre-prepared salads and reheated rice, I carefully cooked each meal. My diabetes gave me quite a scare. I wasn't as invincible as I thought. I needed to look after my boy.

Getting Ready

Adhering to instruction, I thought long and hard about my birth plan. I read books on natural birthing and convinced myself this was for me. I would opt for a natural vaginal birth with no pain relief or intervention. I would be brave. I would be Superwoman!

As a backup plan, though, I decided to prepare for the worst-case scenario. In the event of an emergency caesarean, I would not be able to drive for six weeks. Being on my own, without close friends or family nearby, I needed to consider all the logistics. So I stocked the pantry with enough food to survive a holocaust. And the cupboard was full to the brim with nappies and wipes.

To ensure I had sufficient funds for some time off, I had arranged with my work to continue for as long as possible. As a contractor, I wasn't afforded the luxury of paid maternity leave, so I was careful to manage my money wisely. The plan was to work up to thirty-eight weeks.

Zoe agreed to be my birthing partner. Although nearly three hours away, she was willing to take time off work and stay with me for a few days. I offered my mum the same deal, but she was booked into a gem course. So the plan was for mum to stay for a week before he was expected, and then Zoe would take over after that time.

Baby clothes, baby toys, baby bedding, baby car seat, baby bottles, baby pram, and everything imaginable related to babies was now in my home. I still had a few months to go.

CHAPTER 20

The Final Stretch

Settled into a routine, I mostly worked and slept. I did manage to visit Zoe and George on occasion. They were living together in Yamba, a scenic coastal town in northern NSW. Each day on my trip home from work, I would ring Zoe for our daily debrief. Her life was on track with a new job, a new house being built, and hopes of children in the immediate future. Her life plan was coming to fruition, and I was incredibly happy for her.

But that all changed in February 2011. It was a Thursday, and I was about to get out of bed to get ready for work when the phone rang. It was Zoe.

"It's all a lie," she said, her voice muffled by uncontrollable tears.

Immediately, I sprang into action. "What!"

"It's all been a lie," she repeated through choked up tears. And then she told me that George had been living a double life.

What? How on earth could that be? There was no going to work now. I needed to find out what the heck was going on. I was in complete and total disbelief.

Incidentally a chain of events had occurred that led to the eventual unfolding of George's deceit. For years, it turned out, he had kept two women, each in what they believed was a committed relationship. The details of the story are not for me to tell, but the whole debacle shocked me to the core.

Why had I not seen this? I trusted this man. The lies were just extraordinary. I should have seen the signs, and I should have noticed something was off. I felt like I had failed Zoe.

Needless to say, I was grateful I wasn't a single woman still searching the field trying to find the right man. I was relieved I no longer had to put up with the crap that was out there in the dating world. Thank goodness I was now growing my own bundle of joy. Zoe's experience reinforced my decision to choose the path of solo motherhood. I was definitely on the right journey.

Poor Zoe! She had a world of pain and heartache ahead of her. My focus was temporarily diverted. I had to look after her. I had to pour my energy into helping her get through this ordeal and monitor her well-being.

One More Holiday

For many years, I had promised Mum I would take her on holiday, but the right opportunity had never presented itself until now. Mum is an avid rock collector—a dedicated member of the local lapidary and fossicking club for over a decade. She never knocked back an opportunity to search for gems, often towing her caravan to remote places in Australia to hunt for precious stones. The club organised a trip to Flinders Island, located in the Bass Strait, just north of Tasmania. Mum was thrilled to be going. With her flights requiring her to change planes in Launceston, it was the perfect opportunity to extend her holiday and explore the sights of Tasmania together.

Louisa Pateman

Having spent a previous part of my life travelling back and forth to Tassie, I was happy to reconnect with the island and glad to spend some quality time with Mum. At thirty-four weeks pregnant, I had to carry a medical certificate confirming I was fit to travel. Fortunately, I just made it into the airline's pregnancy cut-off of thirty-six weeks. Phew!

Arriving at the airport with my large pregnant belly, I was excited to hop on the plane. I was a seasoned traveller. What could go wrong? In all my years of overseas travel, I was blessed to say I had never lost my luggage. I'd heard of many people who did, but I prided myself on my good luck. But my luck was about to run out.

Landing at Launceston, I felt a flood of memories come to the fore. I'd certainly had some wonderful experiences there. I hopped off the plane and waited at the small open-air luggage carousel. It wasn't really a carousel; it was a platform trailer driven from the plane carrying everyone's bags. I knew the drill, having been there many times before. I scanned the trailers. No bag. I scanned them again. *Oh dear, this was not looking pretty ...* I waited for the masses to exit the area and scanned yet again. Still no bag. Okay, now I was getting worried.

I was tired and just wanted to get to my hotel. But alas, my bag never arrived. How on earth could they lose my bag on a one-and-a-half-hour flight? Where could it possibly have gone?

My welcome back to Tassie was now tainted. I spent the next hour handing over my personal details to the information desk. Finally, I picked up my hire car and drove to my rustic accommodation. It may as well have been in the middle of nowhere, with no convenience store in sight. It was late in the evening, and the shops would have been closed anyway. Heavily pregnant with no clothes, no toiletries, and twelve hours to wait before I picked up my mum, I decided to undress and go straight to bed.

Early the next morning, I heard a knock on the door. I was naked, as I was saving my only set of clothes in case I had to wear them every day for the next week. "Who is it?" I questioned.

"Your bag has arrived."

Oh, thank goodness for that. I was so grateful for my toothbrush and my deodorant. Clean underwear, fresh breath, combed hair—all sorted, in just enough time to check out and head back to the airport to pick up my mother.

Our itinerary, which I'd prearranged, took us to the popular tourist destinations. After an overnight stopover, we drove to Cradle Mountain National Park. With Dove Lake in the foreground, the scenery was breathtaking.

Stocking our backpacks with essential items, including a picnic lunch, we prepared ourselves to walk the six-kilometre circuit around the lake. We read the signs, got our bearings, and proceeded towards the walking track. We had barely walked twenty metres from the carpark when my heart stopped. I let out a loud shriek and grabbed my belly.

"Mum!" I cried as I stood frozen with fear. Less than two metres in front of me, a black snake slithered slowly across the path. In a complete panic, I couldn't breathe. "Mum!" I yelled louder and then began to cry.

After what seemed like an eternity, the snake slowly meandered into the vegetation, out of sight. But I couldn't stop crying. My life had flashed before my eyes.

Mum was experiencing her own panic. She was convinced I was about to go into labour. With one hundred and fifty kilometres of windy roads between us and the nearest public hospital, this was not the place I wanted to be having my baby.

We walked back to the carpark and sat on a copper log fence. I needed to get my heart rate down and breathe normally. What a close call! After ten minutes of rest, we unwrapped our sandwiches and ate our lunch to calm our nerves.

Settling myself, I decided it was time. I was ready to take on the walk now. But this time, I grabbed a handful of stones and threw them on the ground in front of me as I strolled along, just to make sure the snakes knew I was coming.

Cradle Mountain stood in the distance. The view was stunning. I looked down, and bumbling along beside us was an adorable echidna, shifting his weight from side to side. Aw, how cute … my heart warmed.

The track was well worn, with long sections of raised timber boardwalks. We were making good time, as we were almost at the halfway point. I don't recall what distracted me, but I was walking in front of Mum and somehow, I missed a step on the boardwalk. Before I knew it, I was heading face down onto the timber planks.

My instincts immediately kicked in. As I was falling, I managed to twist my body to protect my baby belly, such that my right side took all of my weight. I then somersaulted off the boardwalk into the water and reeds. It happened in a flash.

And then I was stuck. With my backpack entirely in the water, I was facing upward like an upside-down turtle. My left arm was wedged underneath me, and I couldn't move. In total shock and disbelief, all I could think of was snakes. I needed to get out of the water in case I was bitten by a snake!

But I wasn't moving. My arm was pinned down tight, and I couldn't bear weight. The whole event had happened with no one around us. Thank goodness! I think my damaged pride was hurting the most.

Mum didn't know whether to laugh or cry. "Grab my hand, and I will pull you up," she offered.

"I can't move, Mum. I can't move my left arm." I knew I had done some serious harm.

Between the two us, and without glamour, we got me back up onto the boardwalk. My backside was wet, and my right breast was in agony. But my belly was okay. And I wasn't in labour—yet. An elderly couple walked past and asked if I was okay. "Yes, I'm fine," I insisted. Stubbornness and a crippled ego would not allow me to ask anyone to stop and help. Mum took all the contents of my backpack and put them into hers. Then she took my scarf and made a makeshift sling for my arm.

I sat on the boardwalk for a long time. We were almost halfway, and I knew we had to push on, but I was just waiting for my clothes to dry.

Arm in the sling, I hobbled around the rest of the lake. I could laugh now. I had to; I didn't want to cry. Tasmania certainly wasn't being kind to me.

That evening, at our little bed and breakfast, I took off my clothes to inspect the damage. My right bosom was completely purple—the entire breast, top to bottom, side to side. It was one massive bruise covering half my chest.

The following morning, we explored the Mole Creek Caves, marvelling at the stalagmite and stalactite formations as we made our way through the caverns. Afterwards, we decided to delay our travels and detour back to Launceston hospital.

As I was pregnant, the radiologist was reluctant to perform an X-ray on my arm. But after discussions with a few colleagues, he had my whole body wrapped in a massive lead blanket, about the size of a gymnastics mat, and went ahead with the procedure.

The results came in: I had fractured my elbow. Great! Just what I didn't need! Since it was a joint, I was told they would not apply a plaster. The only treatment was to keep my arm bandaged and in a sling for the next six weeks—and no weight-bearing during that time.

Six weeks? I was having a baby in six weeks! On my own! How was I going to lift my baby? How was I going to bathe and dress my son? And change his nappies?

Plus, I still had to finish up work. How was I going type? How would I drive my car? Too many questions. I couldn't change the situation. I just had to survive.

The roles were reversed for the rest of the trip. Instead of me being the tour guide, Mum was now the driver, the cook, and the bag carrier. I was delegated to the easy job of passenger and navigator. It wasn't all bad.

My flight home alone was challenging. I had to ask for help many times, and upon arriving at Gold Coast Airport, I had to drive my manual car home with one hand, which was very difficult and very illegal. But I got back alive, and the car was intact.

Five more weeks to go, with only one functional arm and no help close by. I was forced to finish up work early. The hardest thing was putting on my underwear; my belly kept getting in the way. And cooking was out—I couldn't use a sharp knife with only one hand. Luckily, I had stored all that extra food in case of a caesarean. I lived off packaged ready-made meals for the next few weeks.

CHAPTER 21

He Arrives

With my due date in sight, I was a fully functioning human again. My check-ups, now weekly, showed the baby was not yet in position. He was in no hurry to make his appearance. At forty weeks, marking the end of my gestation period, my mum flew up to stay with me, hopeful to meet her grandson. The only problem was that he hadn't yet emerged. Mum could only stay with me for a week, as she had commitments with her lapidary club.

Keen for my mum to see my baby boy, I tried to bring on labour. Each day, we took a long brisk walk, doing laps around the neighbourhood park. I wasn't willing to venture too far from home in case I needed urgent transportation. And I was also gulping down chillies and any other spicy food I could hold down. But as each day passed, there was still no baby.

I was now overdue, and my hospital visits increased in frequency. The public hospital was only a few blocks from my house, a comfortable walk if I wasn't nine months pregnant. I had chosen to labour there because of its proximity. But it required sacrificing delivery by my obstetrician, as he had recently elected to cease affiliation with the public hospital. It also meant I no longer had personalised treatment. I had to accept whatever doctor was on duty. It was a lottery.

Four days past my due date, it was time for another check-up. The doctor on duty was a stranger to me, but he was pleasant. With Mum waiting outside, he checked my vitals and determined that my baby was in position, with head engaged. Thank goodness for that! After explaining my desire to have my mother present at the birth, I was given a membrane sweep to attempt to bring on labour—an internal procedure to loosen the amniotic sac membrane from the cervix. *Oh my God, what a seriously uncomfortable experience!* If this was a taste of what was to come, I needed to throw away my dignity right now.

Eight days past due date and still no baby, it was time for Mum to fly home. She took the bus to the airport to save me the hour-and-a-half round trip. I was officially on my own again. Zoe had work commitments so couldn't head north for a couple of days. I only had two more nights of sleep before backup arrived.

Waking the next day, I decided to embrace my last day of pregnancy. The hospital had advised me to book in an induction once I hit ten days overdue. So this was my final twenty-four hours. *Ha* … So many emotions were permeating through my veins: excitement, pride, relief, fear, hope. It was a complete roller-coaster ride. Until it happened …

At 8:55 a.m., I felt pain. *Uh, oh* … Not quite sure if I had imagined it, I calmed myself down and noted the time. Then it happened again. It was 9:05. Holy crap! I think it was a contraction. Yep, there was another one. I was in labour.

I tried to ring Zoe without success. *All good. Don't get upset*, I told myself. Plenty of women around the world have gone through childbirth on their own. I wouldn't be the first. I could do this.

Experiencing labour on my own seemed quite fitting and somewhat ironic. I had chosen this solo path, so why get upset about going through labour alone? *It will be okay. I will be okay. I am a grown woman capable of doing this without a loved one.* Yes, it would have been nice to have company, and yes, it would have been nice to share the experience with someone special. But it was the outcome that mattered most: the baby and motherhood. How I got there wouldn't matter in the end. *It will be okay. Everything is going to be okay. It's just a little hiccup,* I consoled myself. Although I wasn't in pain yet, I needed to figure out a plan to get to the hospital. I didn't want to ring for an ambulance, as this wasn't an emergency and it would be an expensive choice. I continued to time my contractions throughout the day. Still unable to get a hold of Zoe, I wracked my brain to come up with a transport solution.

I was surprisingly calm. I rationalised that if I could get through this day on my own, then surely I could handle being a mum on my own. I didn't waste time getting upset. The situation was cathartic. I chose to do this on my own, and the universe was giving me just what I'd asked for. *I had to laugh.* I was a capable woman. I just needed to focus and think.

By three in the afternoon, my contractions were five minutes apart, so I rang the hospital to let them know I would be arriving soon. My ingenious travel plan (which I later referred to as a moment of insanity) was timed to the second. My bags were packed and by the door. Following a moment of intense pain, then a deep breath, I quickly grabbed my belongings and made my way into the lift and down to the carpark. Stopping just before my car, I endured another moment of intense pain and took another deep breath.

Hopping in my car, I started the engine. Sitting still in the driver's seat, I paused while it happened again. *Breathe in, breathe out* I told myself. Quickly, I reversed the car and navigated two levels of a circuitous underground carpark before making it out onto the local road network. Pulling over to the kerb just in time, I waited for the next wave of pain to pass. I was timing each segment to the second. Off I went again, passing through two sets of traffic lights before indicating my intention to pull over. Finally, I made it to the last leg—I could see the hospital.

Hospital parking was limited and always full. I didn't want to waste time driving around in circles, so I made a decision to park on a side road in a two-hour parking zone. I knew full well I would get a parking fine, but it was a small price to pay for a baby and significantly cheaper than the cost of an ambulance.

I carefully gathered my overnight bag and slowly shuffled into the hospital. I must have looked a sight: a pregnant woman wandering into the hospital on her own, clutching her belly in pain. I can only imagine my facial expressions during each contraction. As I approached the entrance, a compassionate staff member ran towards me pushing an empty wheelchair. Thanking the man, I sat down, and he pushed me to the labour ward in comfort. I felt an immense feeling of relief. *Ah … I'd made it.*

Zoe Arrives

Finally, I was able to contact Zoe, who had been in a conference all day. Immediately she hopped in her car to start the three-hour drive north.

I was taken to a birthing room, and a nurse checked my stats. My contractions were five minutes apart, but I was only one centimetre dilated—not even close. *Argh!* It was now about five in the evening, Zoe was on her way, and I was resting in the birthing bed. The nurse popped her head in every so often to check on me.

After two hours in the birthing suite, the hospital decided they needed the room. It was time to get a wriggle on. The delivery nurse came in and asked if I would like to be induced to bring on labour, explaining I would be given a drip to expedite my dilation and hurry up the process. The only drawback was that my contractions would likely get more painful. *What? Crap. Oh well, I'm here now. Let's get on with it.*

As the nurse was about to prepare the induction, another nurse arrived for a shift changeover. Standing next to me, the departing nurse gave her a rundown of my situation. The new nurse must have been superior, as she quickly refuted the induction and said, "No, we will transfer you to another ward and wait until you are further dilated." I guess there must have been another woman in labour waiting for my birthing suite.

As I was being informed of this new plan, Zoe arrived. Phew! Flustered and apologetic, she immediately took charge of me and spoke to the nurse.

The nurse, acknowledging I now had support, informed Zoe that she would need to take me home. *What? What the heck? What was this crazy nurse talking about? Home? I was at the darn hospital. My contractions were five minutes apart. I was in pain! What was going on?*

The nurse determined that Zoe was capable of looking after me and, as such, wasn't willing to give me a hospital bed. I was undoubtedly beginning to regret using the public hospital system. How can a pregnant woman in labour with contractions five minutes apart be sent home? The nurse must have been suffering from insanity.

But insanity won over. Zoe was forced to take me home and instructed not to return me to the hospital until my contractions were two minutes apart. At around eight that night, we reluctantly left the hospital. I was not happy.

Zoe assisted me in and out of the car and up to my unit. Home again—with no baby! What a complete disaster.

As I was struggling to cope with the pain of the contractions, Zoe convinced me to take a bath. I was not impressed, although I did as I was told, but the pain did not subside. Wriggling around, constantly changing positions, I just couldn't get comfortable. By nine o'clock, I was begging Zoe to take me back. But as instructed, she just kept timing my contractions.

I wailed in pain with each of the contractions, which were currently three minutes apart. Hours passed—that was an extraordinary number of contractions I had to suffer. Finally, I'd had enough. I started to get angry. It was almost midnight, I hadn't eaten, and all I was doing was screaming in pain. Enough was enough. I was getting evil now like I was possessed by Satan. I had no control over my emotions or what came out of my mouth. I demanded to be taken back.

Just after midnight, Zoe rang the hospital to advise that she was bringing me in. Back in the car we hopped. And back to the hospital we drove. Déjà vu—here we go again. Into the birthing suite we went, a different room this time.

I had suffered fifteen hours of contractions by now, and I needed relief. My natural birth plan had been thrown out the window. I wanted gas, and I wanted it fast. Placing the tube inside my mouth, I sucked in as hard as I could. No effect. I tried it again, sucking in air as I had never done before. Still, there was no effect. What was wrong with this machine? Convinced it wasn't working, I asked Zoe to check the device. Every three minutes, in time with my contractions, I attempted to draw in gas. Nothing was making me feel better.

The nurse monitoring my progress declared I was six centimetres dilated—not yet cooked. My goodness, this birthing business was seriously hard work!

More hours passed. At around four in the morning, the nurse suggested I have an epidural, advising that both the baby and I needed to rest. "*Yes!*" I cried. "*Yes, yes, yes!*" Why hadn't they offered this earlier? I was utterly exhausted.

Zoe was surprised that I agreed, given my prior determination to have a natural birth. But after nineteen hours in labour, I wanted drugs. Forget my idealistic aspirations; I just wanted the pain to go away.

I can't remember what the anaesthetist looked like, but I do remember thanking him over and over again. And I remember thinking I wanted to marry him. I was temporarily in love with this stranger who was taking away my pain. How irrational the brain is! A man walks into my room, inserts a needle into my spine, and the next thing I know, I'm willing to marry him. I guess it was an indication of how grateful I was.

The pain dissolved immediately, and I could breathe normally. I was delirious. And I quickly fell asleep for a couple of hours.

I have no idea where Zoe slept, but I hope she was cared for. I was awakened at around seven in the morning and felt so much better. I was numb around my groin. I couldn't feel a thing. I was eight centimetres dilated—two centimetres to go. Without asking, the nurse gave me a drip to induce labour. My baby had been under duress for long enough.

Over the next hour and a half, I relaxed and ate breakfast as the drip did its job. I couldn't feel a thing. I was in heaven.

At 9:45 a.m., I was told it was time. I was ten centimetres dilated, finally! A midwife came in for the birth. With the delivery nurse on one side of me and Zoe on the other, I was told to push. But I couldn't feel a thing; I had no idea if I was pushing. I couldn't feel my muscles contract. I made a few attempts.

"Wait," the midwife instructed. I needed to obey the orders to only push when told to do so.

It seemed to be taking a while. More staff entered the room. "Push," I was told. Still no baby.

A young doctor entered the room and proceeded to insert a suction cup over the baby's head to extract him. Pulling as hard as possible, the doctor stumbled backwards as the suction cup failed. Three attempts, and still no baby. At this stage, it felt like every staff member on shift was in my room. Doctors and nurses were all crowding around my open legs.

After twenty-five hours in labour, I heard, "One more push." And out he came.

First Contact

Looking down, I watched my baby boy as he was lifted into my arms. His skin had a purple tinge, his hair was dark and wet, and his face was all screwed up. He was perfect! He was beautiful. *Aw* … I was in love—madly, deeply, and utterly in love. My heart melted as tears rolled down my cheeks. My body was so full of joy, I felt like it was about to explode.

"Hello, Nicholas," I whispered to my son.

I suddenly felt whole, complete. I can't put into words the depth of my emotions. And I couldn't stop looking at my baby—his tiny fingers, his cute little nose, his squashed little ears. It was the most exhilarating moment of my life.

I laid him on my chest, skin to skin, and he slowly made his way to my nipple. Wow. Nature is such a beautiful thing.

We made it! I had a baby, and I was finally a mum.

First Three Days

Zoe left to get some well-earned sleep back at my apartment, while Bub and I were taken to the maternity ward. I kept my baby on my chest as he cluster-fed for hours—a hungry little boy.

I was sharing a ward with three other women. One was still pregnant and, with her partner by her side, was watching TV loudly and conversing as if they needed hearing aids. Oh, dear! Opposite them was a lady sans baby. She had delivered by caesarean, and her baby was in the nursery. She was spritely and also had her TV on loudly. Across from me was the transition bed, with a couple of women rolling in and out while waiting for a vacant delivery suite.

Beside me was a small hospital cot that looked more like a plastic tub on a metal trolley. Needing to sleep, I slowly manoeuvred Bub into the cot.

"Waah!"

Oh, no. Bub wasn't happy.

"Waah!"

As cute as his cry was, I couldn't leave him in there. Not only did I feel guilty, I also would never be getting any sleep. I picked him up, sat back on my bed, and laid him on my bare chest. He was happy again. Sleep would have to wait.

Hospital beds are high off the ground—well, at least they seem that way when you are worried about a baby falling off. Paranoid that I would drift off to sleep and lose my grip on Bub, I propped up my pillows and sat reclined on the bed with my knees up.

As the nurse came in to check on us, I asked if they would take him to the nursery so I could get some sleep. "No, he needs to sleep in the cot," I was bluntly told. "The nursery is only for special-care babies and those delivered by caesarean. It's the hospital policy."

Okay. So once again, I tried the cot.

"Waah, waah, waah!"

After about two minutes, the televisions in the room were turned up. Clearly, my roommates were not impressed. Great. No sleep for me in the near future.

Outside my ward was the reception desk, another generator of loud noise. I was shattered.

Zoe came back later in the afternoon, and she looked refreshed. I was so grateful to have her. I was also thankful I had no other visitors. I could barely keep my eyes open. Knowing that I had no close friends or family nearby, some work colleagues had offered to drop in, but I politely declined. I was not fit for public viewing.

After twenty-four hours in the maternity ward, without respite and with less than one hour's sleep, I decided I needed to go home. Keen to free up beds, the hospital was supportive. By leaving early, I qualified for home visits from a nurse in the coming days. First, however, I needed to be shown how to bathe my baby.

The portable plastic cot was converted into a bath, and I was shown how to hold Bub and clean him. Woah, this was trickier than it looked. Nervously, I held my wriggling baby as I wiped each adorable skin fold and crevice.

Zoe had kindly collected my illegally parked car, which was fitted with a baby seat, and she came to retrieve us. Finally, we arrived at home sweet home. How nice it felt to bring my baby home!

Zoe stayed with us for the next few days, for which I am eternally thankful.

Nappy changing, breastfeeding, burping, bathing, and changing his clothes—everything was a new experience. I seriously questioned though, the concept of a onesie with an elasticised opening at the back; trying to get a squirming baby into such a contraption was pure torture. I was convinced this was some weird practical joke and someone, somewhere, was having a laugh. The first night was tough. Not knowing how to calm the crying and worried I would wake Zoe or the neighbours, I stood inside my walk-in robe, swaying to-and-fro, hoping to muffle the screams. It was very overwhelming. I was way outside of my comfort zone.

But I survived, and so did Bub. And despite my floundering, every moment was precious. I had never felt so much love and so much joy.

CHAPTER 22

The First Year

Motherhood was blissfull. Every minute of every day, I felt smitten. My beautiful baby boy was laughing, smiling, burping, and crying. Who would have thought such simple things would fill my heart with pride?

Family and friends soon flew up to meet my new arrival.

New Identity

As an SWC35+, my identity had been clear: a single woman, on her own, no husband or dependants. It was a pretty clear categorisation. And my identity was reinforced every time I described my situation to someone new. "I am single, and I want to settle down and have children one day," I would retort. And although I gave this description to myself, I also felt trapped by it.

But now, I had a new identity. Breaking free from my SWC35+ curse, my disease, I now had a new label, a new description. I was now a mum—a single mum. The new identity made me smile. *Mum.* A massive internal shift occurred inside me. I felt mature. I felt responsible. I felt proud. I liked my new identity.

Mothers Groups

The home-care nurse instructed me to visit the local postnatal support drop-in clinic to get regular check-ups and meet other mothers. Each Thursday, I turned up to the centre to get Bub weighed and listen to the weekly pep talk—about breastfeeding, sleeping issues, crying, feeding, and a whole range of topics to educate new mums.

It was here I met some lovely ladies. Some of the women grouped together to form their own mothers groups. And not wanting to offend anyone, I joined not one but two.

It was nice to get out of the house. And it was awesome to make new friends. Some of the mothers were married, some were single, some were old like me (or should I say *mature*), some were young. Some were working, some not.

Opening up about how my son was conceived, I expected some eyebrows to be raised. But no one flinched. How my son came into this world bore no significance. We were one and the same: new mums with our newborn bubs, just wanting to do our best. It didn't matter that I had chosen to become a single mum. I was accepted and welcomed into the fold. I didn't feel like an outcast.

Taking turns, we organised weekly catch-ups in a park, at the beach, or at home doing crafts. Our focus was on our bundles of joy. And we spent hours comparing stories and consoling each other about our sore nipples, pelvic floor loss, stretch marks, saggy boobs, and sleepless nights. We were all on the same page: new mums who loved their little ones, coming together to build friendships.

Back to Work

Heading back to work was always going to be a challenge, emotionally and logistically. Stretching my finances as far as I could,

I was able to take twelve weeks off work. But now it was time to return—fortunately, for only three days per week.

Childcare options were limited. As soon as I had found out I was pregnant, I'd put my name down for the childcare centre located on the ground floor of my office building in Brisbane. But nine months later, there was still no vacancy. I needed an interim solution.

The occasional care centre near my home could offer two days a week. I took my son in for a trial day, which was really a trial for me. As I walked into the centre, my chest was tight, and my breath shortened. I started to feel anxious. I was met by the centre manager, a jolly lady who radiated warmth. After filling out all the necessary paperwork, I was told the processes and introduced to the nursery staff, both friendly women. I was confident they would look after my boy, but I couldn't calm my silent panic. I lingered as long as I could until I was beckoned to leave.

"When can I return?" I asked desperately.

"It's best to leave him here long enough to get settled and get familiar with us and the new environment," the gentle lady replied.

This was going to be a long day. I walked out to my car and sat motionless. I didn't want to leave the carpark. Maybe I could just stay there for a few hours?

Being separated from Bub for the first time was excruciatingly difficult. Back home, I paced back and forth and checked the clock countless times. I only lasted three hours before hopping back in the car and driving back to the centre.

"You're here so soon?" I was asked. Hmm … I'm not so sure I passed my trial.

Two weeks later, the real deal was brutal. Dropping Bub off on my first day back at work was made even harder by the fact that I would be an hour's drive away if something went wrong. But I didn't have a choice. This was my new reality: a working mum who had to rely on childcare.

For six weeks, I spent most of my working day thinking about Bub, feeling a tinge of guilt for leaving him in care. And then one day, when my alarm went off to depart the office in time for the day-care closure, it dawned on me that I hadn't thought about Bub all day. An enormous wave of guilt swept over me. I couldn't believe that six hours had passed without a single thought. I felt a weird sense of shame.

It did get easier. And after six months, a vacancy turned up for the day-care centre in my office building. It was a relief to know Bub was only two floors away.

First Overseas Trip

Finding the courage to venture out as a single mum, I began to push my boundaries as my confidence increased. It was easy to throw Bub in the car along with his pram, his portable cot, his nappies, wipes, baby wraps, bottles, breast pump, and every other piece of infant paraphernalia known to man. Then off we would travel exploring the coast and visiting distant family and friends.

Before getting pregnant, I had purchased tickets to the Rugby World Cup in New Zealand. Zoe and I had been looking forward to the trip, and now my son was joining the party. First, though, I needed to get him a passport. With the stringent rules around passport photos, it wasn't easy. The photographer placed him on a mat on the ground and took a zillion pictures, trying to get one where he didn't smile. He was so darn cute! I was so excited when his passport arrived.

I kept a copy of Bub's birth certificate (which has the father section left blank) with my luggage along with a letter from the fertility clinic stating my child was donor-conceived. I wasn't expecting any trouble getting into New Zealand, but I didn't want to be questioned about the legality of taking my son overseas. I carried this documentation just in case.

The plane ride was stressful. I'd come equipped with bottles, boob, dummy, baby wrap, wipes, and nappies to cater for any scenario. As we took our seats, I immediately cleaned every surface within reach with disinfectant wipes. Then I strategically placed all the equipment in the seat pocket for easy access. I tied the baby wrap to my bra strap and secured Bub on my lap with his special seat belt. What an ordeal!

Paranoid that his ears would burst, I threw him onto my breast as soon as the plane took flight, modestly covering him with my wrap. Three hours later, we landed in Auckland, and I could breathe again. We made it. And we had a fabulous holiday. Zoe was brilliant, embracing Bub and helping to make the trip rewarding and memorable.

The first year flew by with Bub's first smile, his first tooth, first words, first solids, first time crawling, and, topping it all off, walking on his first birthday.

Finding a man was the furthest thing from my mind.

CHAPTER 23

The Search for Answers

My new life was incredibly rewarding. I was enjoying every day. With my bomb disarmed, I could chill out and breathe easily.

I now had time to think about me—to reflect on my past twenty years of dating and search for answers. Why couldn't I find Mr. Right? Where did I go wrong? What was wrong with me?

I began a long journey of self-discovery. I embarked on a series of courses, seminars, and workshops, learning to understand myself and others better. Exposed to new ways of thinking, I heard terms like NLP (neuro-linguistic programming), transformation, values, and beliefs. I loved the learning, and I especially enjoyed meeting interesting people from all over the world and all walks of life.

Inspired and filled with energy, I discovered ways to tackle problems by applying different perspectives, and I gained an appreciation for both the good and bad experiences in my life. What resonated most deeply, however, was the concept of *belief*. What is a belief? How do we get our beliefs? And why are they so hard to shake?

I realised that my beliefs and my view of the world were formed in my childhood and reinforced as I grew. My life plan, my aching desire to find my soulmate, and my quest for my happily-ever-after were all seeded in my mind at a very young age. Rationally, I already knew this, but I never sat down and questioned whether these beliefs were reasonable or right for me. It never occurred to me that I could choose what I believed. I just dutifully accepted society's norms, listened to my elders, and accepted that to succeed in life, I had to find a man, get married, and bear children.

I wish I had known that a belief is a choice. It might have saved me a lot of heartache. Giving up the notion of coexisting with my soulmate was torturous. And equally, I struggled to come to terms with choosing the path of single motherhood. In my eyes, I had failed my life plan, and it tore me to shreds to concede defeat.

As I sat with my baby cradled in my arms, it was hard to imagine life without him. And by no means did I feel like a failure. I was the happiest I had ever been, brimming with love. Time had offered me a new perspective.

I could see now that my childhood beliefs had dictated the boundaries of my adult life. My options were limited—restricted by society, my family, and my friends.

When I changed my views and decided it was okay to become a single mum—choosing to ditch my childhood fairy tales and long-standing traditions—I paved the way to a fulfilled existence. By deciding to believe I would be just fine on my own, I got to experience pregnancy and the joys of motherhood. By restructuring my beliefs, I got to live a more meaningful and more rewarding life.

Coping on My Own

With a new mindset and the ability to see things from different points of view, I was able to reframe my solo parenting. I learnt to lower my expectations. It would be easy to fall into the trap of looking at coupled mums and wishing I had what they had. And with that, I mean a perception of what they had. It's easy to assume that a second parent would help with the chores, help pay the bills, help cook and clean, take care of the baby, and take turns sleeping at night.

I acknowledge that it can be tough as a single parent at times. I don't receive any verbal recognition from a loving partner (mind you, neither do some of my long-term married friends), and it is burdensome not to be able to share the chores and responsibilities. But I made this choice. There are women out there who are single mothers not by their own volition. I knew and accepted this would be a challenge—and a rewarding challenge it is.

To combat any jealousy, disappointment, or frustration associated with not having help from a loving partner, I made a very considered list of expectations that I would live by. I expected to be solely responsible for all the bills, cooking, cleaning, changing nappies, nurturing, entertainment, and logistics. It was all on me. I also expected to have some sleepless nights. And I was okay with all of this.

When I found myself thinking about what I didn't have, I reminded myself of what I did have. And I rephrased my frustration by inserting the words *I get to*: I get to change my son's nappies I get to drop him off and pick him up from childcare. I get to pick up his toys. I get to cook and feed both of us.

I have learnt to enjoy and embrace the little things. Heaven forbid if I didn't get to do these little things. Nappies didn't last forever, and my sleep returned after two years.

So when other mums complained about the lack of help from their significant other, I just smiled at the irony. I never allowed myself to feel frustration. My expectations were always met or even exceeded. I was never angry or bitter that I didn't have help. I was just grateful to be a mum.

Benefits of Choosing Single Motherhood

In contrast to solo mums who find themselves single due to unforeseen circumstances, I am lucky that I have full custody and control of my son. I don't need anyone else's permission.

I see other single mothers who are struggling with their ex-partners in a constant battle of power and control over their children. I don't have those issues. Whatever happens in my life, my son is my responsibility. It is my choice how I parent him. It is my choice if I spoil him or not. There is no negotiating Christmas dinners or school holiday time. He is all mine.

We can travel together and explore the world, just the two of us, without seeking permission. There are no complications.

CHAPTER 24

Eight Years On

My son, Nicholas, is now eight years old. He is a happy, healthy boy who is smothered with love—a cheeky, clever, affectionate, and handsome little man. Of course, I am biased! His smile just lights up my life.

Over the past eight years, I have watched him grow and evolve into a magnificent human. From his first words to his first day at school, I have cherished every moment. As I tuck him into bed each night, his dark brown hair framing his innocent face, he looks at me with his penetrating green eyes and says, "I love you, Mum." A surge of warmth flows through my veins.

"I love you too, my gorgeous boy," I reply. "I love you more than anything else in the world."

He is my companion, my partner in crime, and my travel buddy. My heart is continually bursting with pride. I love our relationship, and I love our life.

After twenty years of trying to find my soulmate, I finally fell madly and utterly in love—with my son. The most important man in my life is sitting right in front of me, eight years old and 145 centimetres high.

Every day, I am grateful for his presence. Each morning, I see his infectious smile and hear him say, "Good morning, Mummy." Every day is a special day.

Yes, we have our hurdles, just like any family. At times, he drives me crazy, and there are times when I am at my wits' end. But an hour later, I am in love again.

Our Family Structure

From a young age, I have explained to my son that there are many different types of families, and he and I, the two of us, make up our family. Some families have a mum and dad, some have two mums or two dads, some blended families have more than one mum and one dad, some families have only one dad, and some families, just like ours, have just one mum. What is most important is the love we share for each other.

Taking heed of the counsellor's advice, I have talked to Nicholas about his origins. I have told him the seed story. When asked about his father, he will matter-of-factly reply that he has no dad. There is no emotion in his voice; he simply states the truth. He will happily go on to explain to any interested party, "Mummy bought a seed from America and planted it in her tummy, and then I grew into a baby and came out her belly button." This has recently been revised to include the part where the seed joins with Mum's egg, and he actually came out Mum's vagina.

"What?" he exclaimed when I explained how he had entered the world. "How did I fit?" he asked with curiosity.

Good question! And one he will never have to experience personally.

Now that he is a little older, I have explained that his existence was made possible because a kind man donated his seed. And that he is a direct result of that one American seed and my egg coming together on that one day in August 2010 to create him. I have been careful to use the term *donor*, not *dad*, as instructed by the counsellor. So far, Nicholas has taken it all in his stride and seems comfortable with how he came to be.

As for the donor, the seed provider, I am incredibly grateful to have been given the ability to create life. One day Nicholas may choose to seek out more information about his origins, or maybe he won't. It will be his choice. For now, the gift of life is more than enough.

CHAPTER 25

Travel for Two

Being a single mum didn't stop me from travelling, although instead of doing adventure tours, I now holiday with my son. We are a great team, and together we have ventured far and wide. Surprisingly, we have found no shortage of people to share our travel experiences with.

Each year, well almost, we have flown to England to visit Patsy, who ended up back in Norwich, the town she grew up in. She married a man she went to school with, and together they have two energetic, fun-loving boys, her youngest the same age as Nicholas. I love visiting Norwich. It is a beautiful city with charming cobbled streets and its own castle.

Patsy lives in a quintessential English cottage. Constructed in the 1500s, it oozes character, with exposed timber beams, working fireplaces, and uneven mudbrick walls, all surrounded by an enormous, sprawling garden—which I like to call a backyard, to Patsy's amusement. As soon as we arrive, I feel at ease, at home.

The perfect host, Patsy is not only welcoming, she always organises a full itinerary of exciting day trips. We have been taken on boat rides through the broads, fun days at adventure parks, picnics by the brook, and trips to the beach (which is very different to what we have in Australia—no waves or red and yellow flags). Each year, she treats us to a "royal tour," visiting various castles, stately houses, and historically significant places. And along the way, she imparts her detailed knowledge of past events and juicy royal scandals. Patsy loves the royals!

On occasion, she has ditched her hubby and, together with our boys, we have taken trips abroad. I am grateful for our friendship, almost twenty years strong, withstanding distance and time. She has certainly played a pivotal role in my life journey.

On our trips to the UK, we have managed to stop over in Hong Kong several times. We love Hong Kong, although I think it's the gifts I buy from the Kowloon night markets that Nicholas loves the most. My friend Ben moved his family there for work, which gives us an excuse to visit. I find the hustle of the busy streets, the constant noise, and the sometimes offensive smells all very fascinating. We love watching the masses herd from place to place and the red junk boats sail on the harbour.

Trips to Hong Kong aren't complete without the culinary treat of freshly steamed dumplings. My mouth waters as I reminisce. Poking my chopstick into the dumpling to release the steam, bathing it in ginger-infused soy sauce before depositing into my mouth ... heaven!

And of course, there is the mandatory day at Disneyland, arriving in the adorable train carriage fitted with Mickey Mouse–shaped windows and handrails. Heeding advice from Ben, we make our way straight to the back of the park to avoid the crowds. And after a long day in the sun—it is always incredibly hot when we visit Hong Kong—we wait for the parade. Seeing Nicholas's face light up as the Disney characters dance past is worth all the effort. In awe, gasping and pointing, his excitement is uncontainable. The parade is the highlight of the day—the jewel in the crown.

Disneyland is also special to me. I always dreamt of going there as a child, but overseas travel was never on the agenda. Growing up, we spent our holidays camping by the beach or a creek with other families. Kids played together and made their own fun—no jumping pillows or organised craft, just pure and simple outdoor activities. We couldn't afford luxuries, and flying was out of the question.

I don't begrudge my mum for not having money, but it did inspire me to make sure I did. When the time came, I wanted to be able to afford to take my child to Disneyland. At times, I feel like I have swung the pendulum too far. Growing up with very little, I may have overcompensated, providing my son with a room full of toys and overseas trips, which may come back to bite me later on. For now, while I can, I will continue to indulge him.

Zoe, My Extended Family

Following that dark day in February 2011, Zoe's life took a new turn. After much contemplation, she decided to follow the same path as me and become a solo mum by choice. She now has two beautiful boys from the same donor—one seven years old, the other two. She is a loving mother and continues to be a supportive friend.

Zoe and I, although living in separate cities, talk almost every day. Even after my years of self-development, she still knows me better than I know myself at times. And together with our boys, we make wonderful travel companions.

Travelling with another mum is easy. We have an implicit acceptance that exploration is a daytime activity to ensure the kids get to bed on time. We have early nights and early mornings and make the most of each day. Over the years, we have taken opportunities to meet up in foreign countries—Latvia, Poland, Slovakia, and Iceland, to name a few. Hopefully, soon we will find the time to get to Fiji.

Holidays with a Twist

My thirst for self-improvement was unquenchable. Following my initial two-year commitment to transformation, I continued to find courses to refine my learnings. I was fortunate to come across a training being held at Club Med on Bintan Island. "The Inner Game of Everything," it was aptly named. Blending an overseas holiday with new knowledge was the perfect combination. Once I found out that Nicholas could be easily cared for in the kids' club, I jumped at the opportunity.

With the help of an incredibly inspirational coach, I learnt to look back at the past events in my life, both good and bad, and truly appreciate how they have helped me live to my highest potential and be the person I am today. I learnt to be grateful for all the bad things that happened in my life because they helped shape who I am.

We were joined by twenty-five interesting people, some married, some single, some with children. The Club Med set-up was brilliant, Nicholas was spoilt at the kids' club while I attended the course, and together we would socialise with the group in the evenings. It was fun and easy to do as a single mum.

Five years in a row, we travelled to Bintan. Arriving in Singapore airport, we would make our way through customs and then get hit with a tsunami of heat and humidity when we exited the building. The one-hour boat ride to the island was always calm, and at our destination, we were greeted by a group of smiling faces offering cold refreshments.

Every time I walked into the open-air foyer, with its timber canopy ceiling, and saw the resort-style pool below, my muscles relaxed, my shoulders slumped, and my stress magically evaporated. With mocktail in hand, I was in my happy place. And Nicholas was always welcomed. Each time we visited, we were never disappointed. We made lifetime friends and created the most fantastic memories.

Together, Nicholas and I have visited fifteen countries, and I have created quite the little traveller. He keeps asking me, "When are we going on a plane again, Mum?" and reminding me that "it's been a long time since we visited Patsy." I need to teach him some patience, although I may have to find someone better equipped to do this!

And now that my son is eight, I may decide to take him on an adventure tour—a family-oriented one. There are even tours designated to single-parent families.

CHAPTER 26

Dating Again

After eight years as a single mum, have I found *the one?*

Becoming a mum didn't stop my desire to have a special man in my life. But it isn't my primary focus anymore. The universe still delivers me the occasional crush, and I still feel sad and rejected at times when my feelings aren't reciprocated. But the energy expended in thinking about men has significantly diminished. I am comfortable being on my own, enjoying motherhood and creating memories with my son.

Motherhood, I can safely say, has put me at peace. My anxiety has gone, and my fear has disappeared. There is no urgency anymore to find my soulmate. The criteria on my list have been reinstated, the bar height has been restored, and I am happy to wait for a compatible partner. I can now enjoy being single. For the first time, I am embracing singledom and not in any rush to change my circumstances. And I no longer feel the pangs of loneliness.

My approach to dating has changed. My headspace is different, and my checklist now includes my son, as his needs are equal to mine. Any prospect must fit into our little family, and vice versa. It's a fraction more complicated, but that's okay, because a significant

185

other is a "nice to have," not an essential. Nicholas and I are perfectly happy just on our own.

The English Potential

It was almost four years since I had been on a date. Ryan lived in England. We had met two years earlier, but only for a brief conversation. Tall with a gorgeous smile, he had an impressive knowledge of facts. But I was mostly drawn to his deep voice; his broad English accent made my heart skip a beat. Talking about geography or history or miscellaneous nonsense, it didn't matter—I was happy just listening to the sound of his voice. Divorced and without children, he was a genuine prospect.

Following a flirtatious encounter and a new friendship on Facebook, I wanted to find out more. Facebook, incidentally, was my new weapon, a new mechanism to rifle through the lives of possible partners before having to commit to a date. How easy it is now to cross-check data and validate a single status. I wish I had been blessed with this tool in my twenties.

Our paths had crossed on a couple of occasions, and I was interested in getting to know him better. I sparked up some courage and sent Ryan a text. I wasn't sure what to expect. I was an Aussie girl only in the country for a few weeks. I didn't want to come across as transient or temporary.

I was driving a hire car from Norwich to Scotland, having said goodbye to Patsy. I was on my way to the Glasgow Commonwealth Games, and of course, I held a spare ticket. I always did, just in case I met someone special. And perhaps Ryan might qualify. I just needed to gauge his interest.

Without hesitation, the texting banter began. Rapport was immediately established, along with giddiness inside. It had been years since I'd had this feeling.

Nicholas had just turned three. Sitting in the child restraint in the back of the car, he was drinking from his sippy cup full of milk. Chocolate milk was his favourite and still is. I would always carry extra chocolate flavouring in case of emergencies—if he fell over, bumped his head, or just couldn't get settled. The magic potion, chocolate milk, cured all.

Choosing to break up the seven-hour drive to Glasgow, I stopped for a couple of nights at the Lake District, in a charming village called Ambleside. Our bed and breakfast was perched on the hillside with views to Windermere, England's largest natural lake. Nicholas was still young enough to sit in a stroller, so the next morning, I strapped him in, and away we went to explore our surroundings.

As a solo mum, it is the logistics that matter the most. "Hands-free," I would repeat to myself whenever I was packing for a trip. Any item that allowed me to be hands-free was a must, which is why I fell in love with my baby carrier. From three months old through to four and a half years, Nicholas rode on my back like a baby Koala. The carrier distributed his weight to my hips, just like a hiking backpack, and clipped together at the front, pulling the weight off my shoulders. It was the most comfortable way to carry him. I loved it. And so did he.

After our tranquil stopover, it was time to continue our journey. I manoeuvred Nicholas back into his car seat and drove north along the winding roads past the crumbling stone fence walls separating the dark green pastures, undulating hills, and peaceful countryside.

Arriving in Glasgow, I was happy to chill out in our spacious accommodation, an old terrace house converted to a bed-and-breakfast-style offering. Our room, with three beds, high ceilings, and a large bay window, would have been a living room before the conversion. Along one wall was a retrofitted bench with enough space to make tea and coffee. But there was no fridge. I couldn't get used to the lack of refrigerators in the UK. I expected a bar fridge—somewhere to keep the milk, chill the drinks, and keep my chocolate bars solid. Alas, it was not deemed a necessary appliance in this part of the world.

Having laid the groundwork, and with my spare ticket in hand and only my pride to lose, I invited Ryan to join us at the games. To my delight, he hopped in his car and drove all the way to Scotland a few days later for three days of fun. Ryan accompanied us to a hockey match, followed by an afternoon at the Green, a live-site bustling with people, food stalls, and outdoor screens showcasing the games. The following day, with the help of a babysitter, Ryan and I watched Australia play New Zealand in the netball final, a nail-biting match to the very end.

Netball was my favourite game, the game I had played since I was seven, and the game that had given me two knee reconstructions and a permanently dislocated shoulder. I loved watching this match. I had seen this head-to-head before, at the Manchester Commonwealth Games and again at the Melbourne Commonwealth Games, where I had snuck in as a staff member using my manager privileges.

Ryan was a gentleman. Although sharing our spacious accommodation, he did not attempt to seduce me. After three days, Nicholas and I waved him goodbye as he drove off in his car. I was smitten.

We stayed in touch. Ever the optimist, I wracked my brain to think of a way I could see him again. In hindsight, I should have let him chase me. I should have forced him to put in more effort. As with my relationship with Alan, I carefully concocted a plan to meet again. It was all my doing.

Nicholas and I flew back home to the Gold Coast, but I was unsettled. We'd enjoyed our time with Ryan, and I wanted more. I had four weeks of work lined up before our annual trip to Bintan Island, which I had booked a year earlier. As hard as I tried, I couldn't align Bintan and the Commonwealth Games. So I conceded we would make two separate trips, and I would work the four weeks in-between.

And then it dawned on me: we would already be halfway across the globe, flying into Singapore. From there, it was a *mere* ten-hour flight to the UK. Maybe we could just keep flying and head back to England?

Ryan and I were in daily contact, texting non-stop and FaceTiming every evening—well, evening for one of us, morning for the other. I desperately wanted to see if this would work. I was fully invested now. And yet, we hadn't even kissed … well, not passionately. Was I mad? Was I utterly insane to even contemplate the idea of getting back on a plane to go all the way around the other side of the planet to visit a boy who didn't even make a move on me when he had the chance?

But he was keen now. His eager replies were proof of that. And we were both intensely excited about the idea of catching up again. But we weren't sure when that would be.

Being the world's most impatient person, I didn't want to wait any longer. I wanted to know now if this almost-relationship was going to work. So I casually tried the idea on for size: "What if I come back to England after my Singapore trip?" I tentatively asked.

It was a go. Ryan was in. I orchestrated another six weeks off work. Technically, I wasn't *off* work—as a contractor, I could do my own hours—but financially, I couldn't be away for too long. I still had to pay the bills.

I managed to arrange some work to take with me. Bargain! I could earn some money, so the trip wouldn't be too financially taxing. And the accommodation would be free. Nicholas and I were about to sample living in South Yorkshire, England.

Deliriously excited, I packed up our ridiculously oversized bags and flew to Singapore. Bintan Island was that much sweeter, as I spent the whole time on cloud nine. I was on my way to love. A piece of my heart had a feeling Ryan might be the one. I was smug and completely chuffed.

After a fabulous ten days in Bintan, Nicholas and I boarded the plane to Manchester Airport. With my son on my back, I collected our luggage and made my way through to the arrivals hall. My heart was pounding. And there Ryan stood, with a mammoth smile on his face. *Hah* ... Everything was going to be great.

The first seventy-two hours were indeed fabulous. Ryan made us feel incredibly welcome and had decked out his spare room with a bed and toys for Nicholas. But three days in, something wasn't quite right. Ryan was affectionate during the day, and our conversations were, as usual, interesting and intellectually satisfying. In the evenings, we would lie together on the couch, watching TV while Nicholas was in bed. It had all the signs of a functioning relationship. But in the bedroom, it all disappeared. Had I done something wrong? Once again, it seemed, I found myself in a relationship with no intimacy. What the hell was I doing wrong?

We took weekend getaways, spent quality time together, held hands, and talked all hours of the night. But that's all. The crucial ingredient was missing. Many times, I raised the question, "What is going on with us?" But Ryan was unable to give an explanation. He didn't understand it himself. He didn't have any answers.

In a strangely comfortable but incredibly sad way, we stuck out the six weeks. I didn't want to leave. Every day, when Ryan returned home from work, I would be sitting in the lounge room with Nicholas, probably watching the *Minions* movie for the hundredth time, and I would notice Ryan at the door. My heart would race. I was so happy he was home. Even with the lack of intimacy, I just enjoyed his company. I spent six weeks on an emotional roller coaster, with massive highs and massive lows. Was this going to get better? Was Ryan just afraid of my living in Australia? I had declared upfront I wanted to eventually settle down in Australia. Should I have been more flexible? And why couldn't he just tell me what was wrong?

Ryan transported us back to the airport. We hugged him goodbye and headed towards the departure gates. We stopped to turn around and wave. As we did, Nicholas let go of my hand and ran straight back to Ryan, giving him a big lingering hug. My heart sank.

When I returned to Oz, our texting stopped. After all, what was the point? Ryan wasn't chasing me. He wasn't telling me he had made a mistake. He stood there at the airport and allowed us to walk away. There was no reason to stay in contact. That would be equivalent to self-inflicted torture. It was time to break free.

A Comfortable Union

I was once again damaged by love. I wasn't interested in dating anymore. Why bother? My heart was totally battered and bruised. I felt a familiar emptiness. Rejection, regardless of how many times I had experienced it, always hurt. The one thing holding me together was my son. My love for him hadn't faltered. How grateful I was to have him in my life.

Nicholas kept me smiling and kept my heart alive. The one man in my life who never let me down was this gorgeous boy in front of me with his cheeky grin and adoring eyes. My little man.

Shortly after Nicholas was born, I had joined a meetup group for single parents. I wasn't sure what to expect. I figured it would be a way to connect with other adults whose priority was their children. We attended several organised events and met some of the regulars. I hadn't formed any lifelong friendships, but it was lovely to hang out with other adults and kids on occasion.

A month after my return from England, the group planned a weekend getaway at a caravan park in Ballina, in Northern New South Wales. The resort-style park came with jumping pillow, swimming pool, and mini-golf. I wasn't ready to socialise, but I needed to get off the couch. I booked a self-contained cabin and decided I wouldn't push myself too far. I didn't have to spend every minute with the group; I would just pop my head in and see how I felt.

And I'm glad I did. Admittedly, I chose not to eat dinner with the twenty-plus group of people. But I did find a few familiar faces by the pool during the day. I couldn't shake my feelings of failure—that, yet again, I was the product of a failed relationship. I wasn't ready to divulge all the gory details. I was too sad.

However, I found solace in listening to two of the other mums. Each had just come away from her own relationship break-up. Both had moved in with their prospective partners, and after trying their best, the relationships had broken down. I wasn't alone. I was so relieved and inappropriately happy to hear about their misfortunes. How evil does that make me? Their stories made me feel normal again. They snapped me back to reality. I wasn't the only woman in the world struggling to hold down a relationship.

That evening, I took Nicholas over to the barbeque area where the group convened. I had no intention of staying. I was just being polite. I said hello to a few other regulars so as not to offend anyone.

Following a quick catch-up, one of the girls casually mentioned that her boss liked me. *What? Where did that comment come from?* Curious, I asked who her boss was. "John," she replied.

I knew who she was referring to. She asked if she could give him my phone number. *What the heck*, I thought. I didn't particularly care. "Sure," I said, never expecting to hear from him.

John and I had met at another meetup event where a group of adults would meet at different restaurants on the coast to sample food and socialise, sans children. John sat opposite me at a Middle Eastern get-together. He was quiet and pleasant—so quiet, I don't recall learning anything about him. With twelve people at our table, we soon shifted seats to talk to other members.

John and I crossed paths again at a camping weekend organised by yet another meetup group. I had gone a little crazy joining several meetup groups once Nicholas was born, as I was searching for opportunities to get out of the house. With my love of camping, I had recently rewarded myself with an eight-man pop-up tent that I could put up and down on my own, with sufficient height inside for me to stand up easily.

The camping trip had occurred earlier in the year, before my trip to the UK. Excited about the opportunity to use my new tent, I convinced Zoe to bring her son and join us for the weekend—in her own tent, though. Eight-man tents really only have enough room for four people, unless you plan on setting up bunk beds. It was spacious enough for the two of us, plus toys and a little room to spare.

By the banks of the Brunswick River, we set up camp. Only a handful of members turned up. I didn't mind. I was there to spend time with Zoe and sleep in my new tent. With all the mod-cons, I set up our own shelter, cooking area, and camp chairs.

Zoe brought her low-rise four-man tent. It was tiny and cumbersome to put up and down. On the first night, we put the boys to bed early, and we weren't far behind. Zoe doesn't drink alcohol, and I only drink on occasion. So we were happy to leave the group and get some zeds.

In the middle of the night, the rain fell. I love the sound of rain, especially when camping. Nature is so raw when you are out in the elements. The weather, good and bad (although the term *bad* is subjective), is all part of the experience. It's something you have no control over; you just adapt. On clear nights, I love looking up at the stars—the millions of white freckles that make up the Milky Way.

Pretty soon after the downpour, I heard the tent zipper open. "Are you awake?" Zoe asked defeatedly.

"Well, I am now," I chuckled.

"Can we please sleep in here?" she asked. "My tent is all wet."

We madly pulled her blow-up mattress into my tent. I was happy to be the saviour and grateful for my fabulous tent.

Camping means different things to different people. For me, when I camp, I want to experience nature and go back to basics. I like to cook my own food on my portable gas barbeque, fill my esky (or icebox for the non-Australians) with enough food and drink for the entire weekend, and stay close to the campsite in the evenings, maybe playing a few games of cards. I enjoy roughing it—leaving behind the creature comforts of home. Camping for me is very relaxing, an opportunity to de-stress.

Not all my friends are like this. For them, camping is an excuse to get together and get intoxicated, and if possible, head straight to the closest pub. Our fellow campers fell into this latter group. They hopped into their cars and headed up to the pub for dinner. John was one of them. He had turned up on his own late in the afternoon, pitched his tent, and joined the others for a meal.

On our second night, Zoe and I joined the others around a campfire. It was here that I had my first real conversation with John, although I still didn't learn much about him. So I was surprised to find out months later that he was interested in me. About a week after giving permission to hand over my phone number, I received a text message from him, asking me out on a date. It felt like an eternity had passed since that camping weekend.

John was a kind man who showed an interest in my son. Our second date was at the local park, where he played with Nicholas on the swings and then piggy-backed him across the sand to the Broadwater, where hundreds of blue jellyfish lay stranded on the water's edge.

John and I had a slow burn. Not wanting to jump straight into another relationship, I was happy to see him once a week and just hang out. John had a very carefree disposition, something I wasn't used to, and I noticed that his presence calmed me down. To be honest, I would never have dated him if I didn't have Nicholas; he didn't tick enough boxes on my original checklist. But that didn't seem to matter now, as my priorities and my desires had changed. I was more interested in companionship and a man who was good with my son. The sparks no longer mattered.

Over time, we developed a steady relationship. John's work kept him busy during the week, which gave me plenty of time alone with Nicholas. We would catch up on weekends and head to the beach or take a bushwalk. There was no urgency, no time pressure. I could just enjoy his company when he was available. He wasn't smothering, and it was a gentle entry back into the dating world.

Ours was a comfortable union. John got on well with my friends and family and occasionally joined us on international travels. But not all the time. My trips to see Patsy remained a girly get-together, as did my holidays with Zoe.

The three of us shared many great times together, including trips to the snowfields, camping, kayaking, and weekends away. At times, I tried to convince myself that the relationship would endure, that we would grow old together. But deep inside, I knew it would never happen, for many reasons. With over a decade gap in our ages, we each wanted different things. Our goals and aspirations were poles apart.

After four years, we called it quits, and Nicholas and I once again became a family of two. It was a smooth transition—easier than I'd expected.

Four years was a massive achievement and a lovely chapter in my life. I don't consider it a failure. I am grateful to have had a decent male role model in my son's life—someone to help teach him how to ride a bike, kick a ball, and pee in a urinal. Our split was amicable. We have caught up on occasion, which has been lovely for Nicholas, who has been a lot more resilient than I expected.

Perhaps I lingered in the relationship longer than I should have, as I was worried about the impact on Nicholas. It did take a few months before he fully understood that John was no longer my boyfriend. Conscious of my son's need for a male role model, some of my guy friends have offered to step up and be present in his life.

Nicholas and I have settled into our own company. The two of us are conquering the world together. "We make a great team, Mum," he told me when I visited his school to help make Christmas craft.

"We make an awesome team, my handsome boy," I firmly stated. "The best team ever."

We are already planning our next adventure. "When are we going to visit Patsy, Mum?" he keeps prodding.

Another chapter has begun, and I am embracing being single. Maybe in a few years, when I am ready, I might just buy an extra ticket to an international sporting event and see what the universe turns up!

CHAPTER 27

No More Life Plan

Twenty-plus years and eight revised life plans later, I am still unmarried. I'm not even close.

When I think about the energy expended in trying to achieve my plan, a myriad of questions come to the fore: *Why was my life plan, my deemed success in life, so heavily dictated by others? Why was there only one plan? Was it a fair plan to follow? Was it worth the twenty years of focus, energy, and heartache?*

In pondering my life plan, the following thoughts entered my head: I was never in full control of the plan, as its success was dependent upon another person. It required two people. I couldn't achieve society's definition of happily-ever-after on my own. And the probability of the plan being a success was logically very low. It required two individuals to be single, at the same place and at the same time, and in the same phase in their lives. It needed them to have similar values and beliefs and be emotionally available. On top of all of this, it required them both to be able to merge their individual life aspirations and goals, be capable of cohabitating, accept each other's faults, and be physically and mentally attracted to one another. Oh, and also have sufficient finances to make a relationship work. *Holy cow!* Looking at this list of ingredients, I realise I never had a chance.

After much contemplation, it was obvious: any hopes and dreams of fulfilling my life plan had to be banished. I needed to take back control of my destiny.

The Epiphany

My life experiences have made me realise that sometimes it can be a difficult challenge for two people to come together as a couple and for both to grow to their full potential. Could I have grown to who I am today if I was only with one partner? I don't know, but I doubt it. That's not to say I wouldn't have been happy and fulfilled in one relationship. But I'm glad, in hindsight, that I didn't have just one.

I grew the most in the periods when I was single. Each relationship gave me something new—a new dimension to my character and a new piece of my jigsaw puzzle. I can't see how I would have evolved and expanded to the degree I have if I only had one romantic partner for my entire adult life. I'm not saying this can't happen, and Aunty and Uncle were proof that it could. But I'm not convinced that everyone can follow this path.

Two individuals coming together with their unique aspirations and development needs, then building a relationship and staying together requires compromise. But how much compromise is too much?

I am grateful that my life ebbed and flowed into different jobs and various locations, meeting different people. By moving around and meeting a spectrum of human beings, I was exposed to events and opportunities I would not have had if I'd stayed in one location with one person.

I don't regret not settling down. After each break-up, my life trajectory changed and my perspective changed. I have decided to believe that it's not better to spend your life with just one person; it's just different. And whether with one partner, many partners, or no partners, it's about finding as much fulfilment as I can with the cards I've been dealt.

Other People's Opinions

Listening to other people's views on what was best for me could have resulted in missing out on some wonderful life experiences. Does it really matter what other people think? Does it matter that my aunt and uncle believed my biggest goal in life was to find a husband, get married young, and grow together? Should I have listened to friends' advice when they said I was too fussy?

As a young adult, I didn't always question the advice given to me by loved ones. I assumed because they loved me, they must know what was best for me. But was the guidance relevant to *me*? Yes, the advice was offered with love and genuine intentions. But was it applicable to *my* life journey? In hindsight, I should have filtered the input through my own values, and I should not have judged myself when I couldn't heed the advice.

I acknowledge now that people gave me advice based on their own life experience and the perspectives they formed from their own beliefs and personal values, all filtered through their unique life journey, in addition to their individual level of courage and risk profile.

How was someone else's advice relatable to *my* journey? It was nice to be given guidance. It was nice to know people cared enough about me to offer help, and I understand the advice came from a place of love. But for me, if I hadn't opened my eyes to opportunities outside of the advice given to me, I wouldn't have my beautiful boy.

I have learnt to trust my intuition and not be heavily influenced by other people. I am now carving out my own path. And I won't be creating any more life plans!

CHAPTER 28

The Courage to Be Single

Is being single all that bad? For years, people consoled me for being on my own and not having anyone to share my life milestones with. Sympathy also stemmed from within. There were many, many times, too many to fathom, when I felt sorry for myself because I wasn't traversing my journey with someone special.

But I have come to realise that my pity was just a state of mind resulting from unmet expectations, comparing myself against society's terms of reference. My friends and family were sad because I didn't meet their own aspirations. Everyone expected me to accomplish a common dream, and when I wasn't able to bring that dream to fruition, it was natural they were disappointed.

Fortunately, I discovered that I don't need to adopt others' way of life, and I can create my own dreams and my own beliefs. I can set my own terms of reference.

Defining Failure

Each time my relationships ended, I felt like a failure, and this was reflected in the words I used to describe myself. Break-up after break-up, the term *failure* was slowly but surely embedded into my identity. The words I chose had a powerful effect. Using the expression *my relationship failed* did not help my self-esteem, and it reinforced in my mind that being in a relationship was the be-all and end-all of life, the primary measure of my life's success.

In retrospect, if I had fun times and came away with wonderful memories, was the relationship, in fact, a failure? It was only so if I believed it was supposed to last forever. Perhaps I just needed to change my perceptions.

I look at my life now and realise that being single is not a negative. I also believe that leaving an unhappy or toxic relationship to venture out on your own is brave. It requires self-love.

In tough times, I have tried to follow my own mantra: "You determine your own worth by what you will and won't put up with." In my darkest hours, I had to remind myself that I am worthy of a good man and a nurturing relationship. And although it was painful and scary (and possibly delayed at times), I had to cut loose some duds to follow my own advice. I need to be proud of myself for that.

Over the decades, I have seen many friends and colleagues stay in unhealthy and unfulfilling relationships because it was their status quo. They didn't walk away because they didn't know any different. And society pressured them into staying. They didn't want the stigma of a failed relationship and were perhaps afraid to be single. For a multitude of reasons, they convinced themselves they should stay and stick it out, and it would get better. I'm sure for some, it did. I appreciate that relationships ebb and flow, have ups and downs—that's normal. But what if you can't be or grow into the person you want to be?

I have seen desperately unhappy people become bitter and resentful, living out *Groundhog Day* because they didn't possess the courage to be single. Remembering this reassures me that it is okay to be on my own.

No one is more trapped than a person who is living in an unhappy marriage. Don was a reminder of that. I'm not promoting divorce; I acknowledge it's tough, and I appreciate that the end rewards are worth the effort. But I do believe that some relationships, no matter how hard you try, will never go the distance. Sometimes two people need to take different journeys, and sometimes one outgrows the other.

As a single woman, I have hope. I have optimism. I have a clean slate, and I have the excitement of the unknown.

Benefits of Being Single

So it's okay to be single, and it's okay to be in a relationship. Neither is a success nor a failure. They are just ways of being, and there are benefits to both.

Admittedly, being single can get very lonely, and it definitely plays havoc with your self-worth at times. But it also has its advantages. Being on my own allowed me the time and energy to devote to my girlfriends.

For years, I was upset that I didn't have someone permanent to share stories with later in life. But in reality, I did have someone permanent. I had more than one person; I had many. I did get to create memories with people I can reminisce with. Those people just happened to be my girlfriends. If being single meant I got to share adventures with Zoe, Patsy, Maxine, and Judy, then I am blessed. In hindsight, I wouldn't trade any of those experiences for any man.

I never intended to live my life on my own, but my years of being single incidentally taught me to be confident, independent, and resilient. The idea of doing something on my own now is less daunting than it was twenty years ago, as I have proved to myself, time and time again, that I can succeed without a life partner. I can live an exciting and rewarding life, just on my own.

With almost thirty years of adult life behind me, I can finally appreciate being single. I can embrace it and even love it. My goal in life now isn't to find Mr. Right. My goal is to be happy in whatever form that takes. For the foreseeable future, spending quality time with my son is everything I could ask for.

CHAPTER 29

Best Decision of My Life

I never thought I would be so happy to admit I had failed to find a husband. When I look back at my broken relationships and the ones that didn't get off the ground, I am reminded of how lucky I am. So what did happen to all those duds? Fortunately, I didn't keep in touch with most. I didn't have to see them go on to marry other women.

Ross, I believe, went forth and "experienced other women" over the next decade. Eventually, he settled down, got married, and had children. I am thankful he gave me Zoe. I couldn't ask for more than that.

Jim married his next girlfriend after me.

David found it hard to let go, and for months he would send me fresh flowers. I'm sad I broke his heart. He was incredibly sweet, but I don't regret settling for a lifetime without intimacy.

Hugh married Kristin. I have no idea how that turned out, but I hope it was boring.

Dan contacted me about a year after our saga, wanting to touch base, I suppose. I was living in England, dating Trent, but I was reluctant to divulge my personal status. We exchanged a few emails. I was curious to learn why he had reignited contact and was wary of his lack of transparency. Eventually, I extracted from him that he was still with Antonella, and they had just bought a house together. I deduced he was unhappy but lacked the courage to get himself out of the relationship. I felt sorry for him, but not sorry enough to stay in contact.

A few years later, I bumped into him one night at the Slip Inn, the tavern where Mary, Crown Princess of Denmark met her Danish prince. We caught eyes across the crowded room, so I beelined over to say hello. He looked surprised to see me; actually, scared and stunned would be a better description. We exchanged very quick courtesies before I asked, "How's Antonella?"

To which he replied, "We got married, and she's outside now. I have to go." He couldn't run away fast enough.

Thankfully, I never saw Trent ever again. And until writing this book, I had carefully extracted him from my memory.

Don … well, it took him seven years to leave the marital home. Seven years! Once a year, or thereabouts, he would orchestrate a dinner together to catch up. It was nice to see him and reminisce, but his intentions were always the same. He wanted "benefits," and I wasn't willing to give them. I was over him romantically. Once I had my son, the dinners stopped, and I have not seen him since.

I have no idea of Luigi's whereabouts and no desire to find out.

Alan went on to meet the love of his life shortly after we broke up and soon after got married. We don't keep in touch, but I hope he is happy. It took me a long time to reconcile my decision to leave him. It helped that he moved on so quickly, somewhat validating my actions.

Jeff … I have fond memories of Jeff. But we just weren't compatible. I have no idea if he married for a third time or if he changed his mind about children.

Towel guy—argh! Just writing about him makes me cringe. I want to erase that memory. I have no idea how he ended up; I'm just glad it wasn't with me. I still feel like I dodged a bullet.

As for my English love, Ryan, we haven't seen each other or spoken in five years. I can reconcile now that it wasn't meant to be. And finally, John and I have remained friends, and that is nice, especially for my son. I wish him well.

I can comfortably say with complete conviction that I am so very grateful my relationships ended. If I hadn't dated an array of duds, I wouldn't have created my gorgeous boy. And now I am free to build memories with my son, the one true love of my life.

No More Waiting

As I pull together the pieces of my journey thus far, I can see that each chapter brought something new. Together, those chapters have made me who I am today.

Thank goodness I didn't wait around for my soulmate to cross my path. I have lived an extraordinary life by accepting (sometimes reluctantly) what was in front of me, even though I longed inside for Mr. Right. I am proud of myself for buying a home and travelling overseas on my own, but initially, these things were incredibly hard to do, purely because I had a subconscious belief that I was supposed to do those things with my soulmate. I am so glad I plucked up the courage to progress in life alone. I would have missed out on a lot of joy if I was still sitting on my couch pining for the love of a man.

If I had waited for *the one*, I would never have had the most exciting and rewarding life experiences.

Last Words

Thus far, I have lived a wonderful life, although I didn't follow the path set for me by society. I didn't meet my soulmate. I didn't find the right man to settle down with. And yet I feel incredibly lucky. I am deeply appreciative of what I do have. At twenty-five, I could never have imagined how happy I would be in twenty years, knowing I wouldn't follow my life plan.

I have had a great career. I have travelled to numerous countries. I have met many interesting and inspiring people. I have created the most amazing memories.

There are so many things I am grateful for. Incidentally, I live in a country that offers assisted fertility services to single women. I was shocked to find there are countries I consider progressive that don't even allow it. How lucky I am.

I am grateful for my life experiences, good and bad. During my moments of heartbreak, or heart-bruising, I was temporarily consumed with sadness and despair, but I always bounced back. And although it was often painful, I found a way to move on. I forged ahead and kept creating new memories, and in the end, I got to be a mum.

As for being single now, I have hope and optimism and the excitement of the unknown. I have courage and a belief that I can continue to create happy adventures regardless of my status. And most importantly, I get to love my boy, nurture and guide him, and watch him grow.

In retrospect, my thirty-year pursuit of my happily-ever-after was a definite fail—based on the traditional connotations of the term. And that's okay, because it's just an abstract notion, a throwaway line, a simple, concise sentence to wrap up a fairy tale: "And they all went on to live happily ever after. The end."

Sadly, the happily-ever-after notion is deeply embedded in the subconscious mind of many a young girl and older ones, too—so deep, in fact, that it is almost impossible to remove. Imagine if the fairy tales or books we read as children had more empowering messages?

Imagine how much happier and freer young women would feel if they had a deeply embedded notion of choice, of carving out their own unique path? Imagine how liberated young women would be if society bestowed upon them a belief that you don't need to wait for your Prince Charming, that you can create an extraordinary life just on your own?

Oh well … maybe one day.

As for me, I made the best decision of my life. I chose a different path and went on to have exciting and rewarding life experiences forever after. The end.

AFTERWORD

It was a difficult decision to bare my life and soul for the world to see my failures and judge me. I acknowledge people will assess me according to their beliefs and their values, and that's okay. It is highly likely I won't share their views. Beliefs are, after all, a choice.

My failures are only failures if you subscribe to the notion of only one life plan, one predetermined path of marriage followed by children. If you allow yourself to be open to the idea of alternative paths, different beliefs, and the concept of setting your own unique journey, then I haven't failed.

Initially, I worried about the effect that writing my memoir might have on my son. Interestingly, Nicholas, knowing that "Mum is writing a book," has been inspired to write one too. He comes home from after-school care with pages of text to add to his book about various villains and plots he has conjured up. If writing my memoir does nothing else, I am pleased I have sparked his interest in becoming an author.

After being asked by colleagues and co-workers, who know about my solo motherhood endeavor, if I could talk to their daughter, their sister, or even themselves, I decided to write my story. There is a lot of curiosity on the topic, and many people don't realise it is an option—yet there are thousands of women who have taken this path, from all around the globe.

If just one woman can relate to my story and find comfort in knowing she is not alone, then I am happy. And maybe, just maybe, if I inspire one SWC35+ to challenge society's norms, take back control of her destiny, and choose the path of single motherhood, then writing this book has been well worthwhile.

Printed in the United States
By Bookmasters